Grains, Rice, and Beans

KEVIN GRAHAM

Grains, Rice, and Beans

Photographs by

ELLEN SILVERMAN

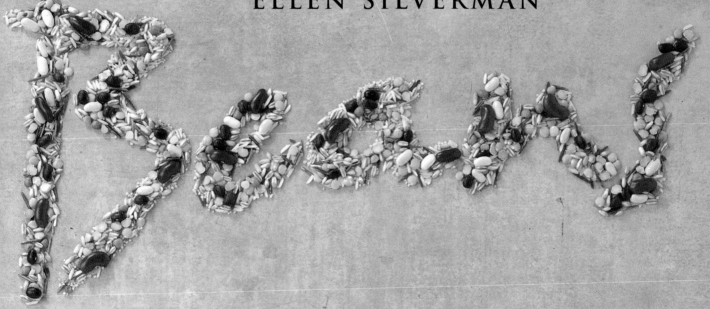

ARTISAN
NEW YORK

To Tom Cowman and Jean Mestriner

EDITOR: Melanie Falick
PRODUCTION DIRECTOR: Hope Koturo

Published in 1995 by Artisan
a Division of Workman
Publishing Company, Inc.
708 Broadway, New York, NY 10003

LIBRARY OF CONGRESS
CATALOGING-IN-PUBLICATION DATA

Graham, Kevin.
Grains, rice, and beans / Kevin Graham;
photographs by Ellen Silverman.

    p.   cm.

ISBN 1-57965-127-5
1. Cookery (Cereals) 2. Grain.
3. Cookery (Beans) 4. Beans. 5. Cookery
(Rice) 6. Rice.   I. Title.
TX808.G72   1995
641.6'31—dc20   94-45986
                CIP

Printed in Japan
10 9 8 7 6 5 4 3 2

CONTENTS

GRAINS, RICE, AND BEANS *are the original dietary staple. For thousands of years, these wholesome and readily available foodstuffs have played key roles in the sustenance of human beings and animals. But as societies have gained wealth, the people within them have often moved away from eating these foods. Meat, particularly beef, has taken on more prominence in affluent diets, while the more earth-based grains, rice, and beans, foods that can usually feed a lot of people for a small amount of money, have been relegated to the role of peasant cuisine. Somewhere along the culinary road, our society lost its appreciation for the high-quality nutrients and flavor these ingredients bring to our table.*

From the time I started traveling to different parts of the world as a young man, I have always been struck by the universality of grains, rice, and beans. They are featured in national and regional specialties around the globe and, because they remain the "food of the people," such dishes often retain unique flavors that are distinctly indicative of their culture: couscous in North Africa; polenta, risotto, and pasta in Italy; kasha in Russia; grits in the American South; dhal in India; ful in Egypt; sushi in Japan. Many of these recipes have been with us since the dawn of civilization, relatively unchanged in their basic ingredients.

Today we are rediscovering both the flavor and the healthful benefits of these foods. We know that while meat can be good for us in small quantities, ounce for ounce, beans, rice, and grains are far better sources of complex carbohydrates, fiber, and many vitamins. And, when eaten in certain easy-to-make combinations (such as rice matched with beans), they are also an excellent source of protein. We also know that cultivating grains, rice, and beans is far more land efficient than raising animals for human consumption. According to the Wellness Encyclopedia of Food and Nutrition, *the amount of land required to raise enough beef to feed one person can yield enough wheat to feed 15 people or enough rice to nourish 24.*

The choice to follow a vegetarian diet is a personal one. I am not a vegetarian and I am not advocating or discouraging such a diet here. However, I do believe that moderating meat consumption while increasing the consumption of beans, rice, and grains as well as nuts and seeds helps us to maintain our own health as well as the health of our planet.

This is not an all-encompassing compendium on beans, grains, nuts, and seeds nor is it a book of so-called "health food." Rather, it is a personal collection of my favorite recipes and the dishes that are most popular among my friends and family as well as guests at my restaurant. The recipes in this book demonstrate how beans, rice, and grains can be incorporated into each part of the meal, from appetizers to meatless main dishes to side dishes to desserts. Many of the recipes are low in fat, not because I skimped, but because I focused on bringing out natural flavors rather than cushioning food in fats.

To save on fat, frequently I use beans and lentils instead of flour-butter mixtures as thickening agents in soups, sauces, and dressing; when I make bean dishes, I tend to take out the traditional pork fat or simply replace it with a more healthful alternative, such as smoked chicken. I still use such gratifying ingredients as Gorgonzola and Mascarpone cheeses, as well as chocolate in my recipes, I just use them in moderation. My philosophy of cooking—and eating—has nothing to do with denial but is based on an awareness of how food makes us feel. It is a simple, light way of nourishing ourselves that gratifies not only our sense of taste, but also our sensitivity to smell, temperature, texture, and visual beauty.

The recipes range from my interpretations of classics like Walnut Scones (page 164), Italian inspired risottos, and Peanut Soup (page 153) from Asia and Africa, to recipes that combine different cultural influences, such as Wasabi-Sesame Rice Cakes with Mascarpone Dip (pages 128–129), which I was inspired to create after watching Japanese chefs make sushi with sticky short-grain rice. There is a Brandade of Navy Beans (page 42), in which I replace the traditional salt cod with a white bean purée; and Wheat Berries with Rice Wine Vinegar and Raspberries (page 100), an exciting combination of diverse flavors and textures.

I hope you will enjoy making the recipes here and, after reading about the beans, grains, nuts, and seeds that I've highlighted, you will seek out and create new ways to bring these ingredients to your table frequently. Beans, rice, and grains are fascinating to me as much for their great taste, versatility, and healthfulness as for their role in the lore of civilizations. This book is proof that discovering something new is often about rediscovering something old.

Beans

Top, left to right: fava beans,

navy beans,

corona beans

Middle: dried cranberry beans,

fresh cranberry beans,

flageolet beans,

scarlet runner beans

Bottom: mung beans,

pavom (rattlesnake) beans,

borlotti beans *(above),*

black beans

Top, left to right: miso,

pinto beans,

haricots verts

Bottom: red kidney beans,

large lima beans,

baby lima beans,

tofu

KIDNEY BEANS
AND OTHER RED BEANS

Kidney beans are believed to have originated in Mexico over 5,000 years ago. Named for their shape, they are approximately $\frac{1}{2}$ inch long and range in color from dark reddish brown to pale red to white (when white, they are called cannellini beans). Also available are immature pale green kidney beans known as flageolets.

Red kidney beans should not be confused with small red beans, which are smaller, dark red ovals, or with adzuki beans, even smaller red ovals marked with a fine white line. Both red kidney beans and small red beans are used to make chile con carne as well as red beans and rice, though it is the small red beans that are considered most traditional for these dishes. Adzuki beans are the key ingredient in red bean paste (a mixture of mashed red beans, shortening, and sugar), which is used to make many Asian sweets. Cannellini beans are especially popular in central Italy, Greece, and France.

Kidney Beans

For the quintessential New Orleans Monday supper, liberally splash the beans with hot pepper sauce and serve them with steamed rice, garlic bread, and a tossed green salad. To give the beans more body and flavor, add diced leeks, carrots, or any other vegetable 15 minutes before the beans finish cooking.

• 1 cup dried kidney beans	• 1 teaspoon olive oil
• 6 cups Chicken Stock (see page 181) or Vegetable Stock (see page 180)	• 1 medium bay leaf
	• 1 sprig fresh thyme
	• 2 cloves garlic, peeled and minced
• 1 large yellow onion, peeled and finely chopped	• $\frac{1}{2}$ teaspoon freshly ground black pepper
	• 1 teaspoon salt

Place the beans in a colander and pick over to remove any stones or discolored beans. Put the beans in a large stockpot, cover with fresh cold water, and soak for at least 3 hours or preferably overnight to expedite the cooking process.

Drain the beans and return to the stockpot. Add the remaining ingredients to the pot and cook gently, uncovered, over medium-low heat until the beans are tender, about 45 minutes to 1 hour, skimming the surface occasionally to remove any scum that may have risen to the surface. If necessary, drain the beans to get rid of excess liquid. Discard the bay leaf and serve.

Makes 2¼ cups

Kidney Bean Soup with Chopped Shrimp and Chicken

THE CONSISTENCY OF THIS SOUP tends to be thick, so it can be served as either an appetizer or a main course. It can be made with just shrimp or chicken if both are not available or desired. Accompany with warm garlic bread.

- *2 tablespoons canola oil*
- *2 large yellow onions, peeled and finely diced*
- *1 clove garlic, peeled and minced*
- *1 medium bay leaf*
- *3 cups cooked kidney beans (see page 11)*
- *Pinch of cayenne pepper*
- *8 cups Chicken Stock (see page 181) or Vegetable Stock (see page 180)*
- *1 cup diced raw chicken breast*
- *1 cup peeled and deveined small raw shrimp*
- *1 cup peeled, seeded, and diced tomato*
- *1 cup steamed rice*

Heat the oil in a heavy stockpot over medium-high heat. Add the onion, garlic, and bay leaf, and sauté for 5 minutes, stirring continuously. Add the beans and cayenne pepper and sauté for an additional 3 minutes. Add the stock and bring to a boil. Reduce the heat, cover, and simmer for 1 hour, stirring occasionally, until the beans start to break down, thickening the soup.

Add the diced chicken, return the mixture to a boil, and simmer for 2 minutes. Add the shrimp, return the mixture to a boil, and simmer for 2 minutes. Lower the heat, add the tomatoes and rice, stirring well to incorporate, and continue cooking for 2 additional minutes. Remove the soup from the heat and serve.

8 appetizer or 4 main course servings

Flageolet Beans with Roasted Zucchini

IN MY OPINION, FLAGEOLETS (pale green kidney beans) are the best-tasting of all beans. Here I combine them with roasted zucchini, but you can substitute any kind of squash or eggplant. Be sure not to overcook the zucchini as it is meant to be in crisp contrast to the creamy beans.

I also like to prepare flageolets in the classic Provençal style—with tomatoes, garlic, and herbes de Provence—and in chicken broth with puréed roasted garlic.

- 1 cup dried green flageolet beans
- 1 large yellow onion, chopped
- 2 large cloves garlic, minced
- 2 medium bay leaves
- Pinch of dried thyme
- 1 teaspoon salt
- 1 teaspoon freshly ground black pepper
- 3 tablespoons olive oil
- 1 quart Chicken Stock (see page 181)
- 6 shallots, peeled and minced
- 1 large tomato, peeled, seeded, and finely diced
- ½ cup dry white wine
- 4 medium zucchini, washed and trimmed
- ¼ cup grated Parmesan cheese

Place the beans in a mixing bowl and cover with cold water. Allow to soak for 3 hours, then drain.

Into a large saucepan, place the soaked beans, onion, 1 clove garlic, 1 bay leaf, thyme, ½ teaspoon each salt and pepper, 1 tablespoon olive oil, and the chicken stock. Bring to a boil, reduce the heat, cover, and simmer until the beans are tender, approximately 45 minutes to 1 hour, skimming the surface of the stock from time to time to remove any scum that may have formed.

Drain the beans, discarding the stock and bay leaf, and allow to cool.

In a separate saucepan, heat 1 tablespoon olive oil. Add the remaining clove of garlic and the shallots and sauté until soft, about 2 minutes. Add the remaining bay leaf and the tomatoes and sauté over high heat for 2 minutes. Add the wine and reduce the mixture by half. Remove the pan from the heat and slowly fold in the cooked beans. Season with salt and pepper. Set the pan aside and cover to keep warm.

Preheat the oven to 450° F.

Split each zucchini in half lengthwise. Brush with the remaining olive oil, season with the remaining salt and pepper, and lay on a baking sheet skin-side down. Bake in the oven for 10 minutes. Allow to cool.

Cut the halved zucchini crosswise into ¼-inch slices. Divide the slices among 4 serving plates, shingling the slices to form a 4-inch galette (round) on each plate. Spoon a fourth of the beans into the middle of each zucchini round and top each serving with a sprinkling of grated Parmesan cheese.

4 appetizer servings

Kidney Beans
with Smoked Chicken

UNSMOKED CHICKEN MAY BE SUBSTITUTED in this recipe, but the flavor will not be as intense. The rendered chicken fat in which the beans and vegetables are cooked lends another dimension to the pleasant, smoky flavor of this dish.

Place the beans in a colander and pick over to remove any stones or discolored beans. Put the beans in a large bowl, cover with fresh cold water, and soak for at least 3 hours or preferably overnight to expedite the cooking process.

Place the chicken on a large cutting board. Pull off the legs, remove the skin, and pick the meat from the bones. Reserve the meat and skin. Carefully remove the skin from the rest of the chicken and place with the skin from the legs. With a sharp knife make a cut down the length of the breast on both sides of the breast bone. Remove the meat by pulling backward from the wishbone. Place the white meat from the carcass with the leg meat, cut into bite-sized pieces, and set aside. Discard the bones or reserve to make a stock.

- *2 cups dried kidney beans*
- *1 whole smoked chicken (3 to 4 pounds)*
- *2 tablespoons canola oil*
- *1 large yellow onion, peeled and diced*
- *1 large green bell pepper, cored, seeded, and diced*
- *1 medium bay leaf*
- *2 stalks celery, trimmed and finely chopped*
- *4 cloves garlic, peeled and minced*
- *½ teaspoon freshly ground black pepper*
- *1 teaspoon salt*
- *4 cups boiled white rice (for serving)*

Place the chicken skin with the oil in a large, heavy stockpot and sauté over medium-high heat for about 2 minutes to render the fat. Remove the skin and discard. Add the onion, bell pepper, bay leaf, celery, and garlic to the rendered oil and sauté until the vegetables are soft, about 5 minutes.

Drain the beans and add to the pot with the vegetables, covering with fresh water to about 1 inch above the beans. Bring to a simmer and cook gently, uncovered, over medium-low heat for 45 minutes, skimming the surface from time to time to remove any scum that may have formed on the surface.

Add the chicken meat and spices to the red beans and continue cooking for an additional 15 minutes or longer, until the beans are tender.

Remove the pot from the heat, discard the bay leaf, and serve Kidney Beans with Smoked Chicken over the rice.

6 main course servings

Kidney Beans with Sherry and Grilled Red Onions

THIS DISH CAN BE SERVED either warm or cold, as an appetizer or entrée. The combination of the sherry, olive oil, and vinegar used to dress the beans with the sweet red onions creates a mild, enticing sweet-and-sour effect.

Place the beans in a colander and pick over to remove any stones or discolored beans. Put the beans in a large stockpot, cover with fresh cold water, and soak for 3 hours or preferably overnight to expedite the cooking process.

Drain the beans, return them to the stockpot, and cover with fresh water. Using the clove as a pin, attach the bay leaf to the whole onion. Add the vegetable oil, studded onion, garlic, and spices to the pot and cook gently, uncovered, over medium-low heat until the beans are tender, about 45 minutes to 1 hour. Drain the beans to get rid of excess liquid, then return the beans to the pot. Discard the bay leaf, clove, and whole onion. Add the sherry, oil, and vinegar to the beans and stir well to incorporate. Cover and keep warm. Serve with Grilled Red Onions.

4 appetizer or 2 main course servings

- *2 cups dried kidney beans*
- *1 clove*
- *1 medium bay leaf*
- *1 large yellow onion, peeled*
- *1 tablespoon vegetable oil*
- *2 cloves garlic, peeled and minced*
- *½ teaspoon freshly ground black pepper*
- *1 teaspoon salt*
- *½ teaspoon red pepper flakes*
- *2 cups dry sherry*
- *½ cup olive oil*
- *½ cup champagne vinegar (apple cider or malt vinegar may be substituted)*
- *Grilled Red Onions (recipe follows)*

grilled red onions

- *2 large red Bermuda onions, peeled*
- *¼ cup sherry*
- *¼ cup sugar*

With a sharp knife cut each onion crosswise into 6 slices, being careful to keep the rings together. Pin each ring together with a wooden skewer or long toothpick. Place the onion rings in a shallow baking dish and set aside.

Warm the sherry in a small saucepan over low heat, add the sugar, and stir until dissolved. Remove from the heat and pour over the onion rings. Allow the onions to marinate for 20 minutes.

Bring a grill or griddle up to a high temperature (coals on a grill should be grayish white and a griddle should be just below smoking). Place the onions on the grill or griddle in a single layer and cook until well marked, about 3 minutes. Turn and cook the second side. Repeat with the remaining onions, keeping the cooked ones warm.

Remove the wooden skewers and serve the onions as an accompaniment to the Kidney Beans with Sherry.

CRANBERRY BEANS

This tannish pink bean with wine-colored speckles is reminiscent of the pinto bean in shape and has a creamy texture and a distinctive chestnutlike flavor that blends readily with a variety of seasonings. It is the traditional bean used to make the Venetian pasta and bean soup called pasta e fagioli *and is also favored for succotash by some New Englanders. In Indiana and Ohio, it is known as the shellout or shelly bean and is cooked and seasoned with such spices as nutmeg and cinnamon.*

Fresh cranberry beans in their burgundy-striped pods are available in some markets during the spring and summer; shelled cranberry beans freeze well. Dried cranberry beans are an acceptable substitute.

Cranberry beans are also known as Roman beans, borlotti, and coronas.

Cranberry Beans and Asparagus with Herbed Vinaigrette and Parma Ham Crisps

THE CREAMY MILDNESS OF THE BEANS and the tenderness of asparagus tips are juxtaposed in this recipe with the tart, herbaceous vinaigrette and the crunchy, smoky Parma Ham Crisps.

This dish gets better if allowed to marinate for a day or so in the refrigerator, although it doesn't usually last that long around my house. I like to serve it with grilled fish or poultry.

- *1 pound fresh asparagus*
- *1 tablespoon extra-virgin olive oil*
- *1 large yellow onion, peeled and finely diced*
- *1 medium bay leaf*
- *Pinch of salt*
- *½ teaspoon red pepper flakes*
- *1 cup dried cranberry beans*
- *4 cups Chicken Stock (see page 181)*
- *Herbed Vinaigrette (recipe follows)*
- *Parma Ham Crisps (recipe follows)*

Cut the tips from the asparagus and reserve the stalks for another use, such as soup. Boil a quart of salted water in a heavy pot. Drop in the asparagus tips and allow the water to return to a boil. Blanch the asparagus for 3 minutes. Remove the pot from the heat, drain, then shock the asparagus in iced water. Drain and set aside.

Heat the oil in a heavy saucepan over high heat. Add the onion and sauté until soft, about 3 minutes. Add the bay leaf, salt, red pepper flakes, beans, and stock, and bring to a rolling boil. Reduce the heat to a simmer, cover, and cook the beans until tender, approximately 45 minutes. Remove pan from heat and drain. While the beans are still warm, add the asparagus and toss with the Herbed Vinaigrette.

Divide the dressed Cranberry Beans and Asparagus among 4 or 6 serving plates and top each portion with crumbled Parma Ham Crisps. Serve immediately while the salad is still warm or allow to marinate in the refrigerator.

6 appetizer or 4 main course servings

herbed vinaigrette

- ½ cup balsamic vinegar
- ¼ cup olive oil
- 1 small carrot, peeled and finely diced
- ¼ red Bermuda onion, peeled and finely diced
- 1 clove garlic, peeled and minced
- 1 tablespoon minced fresh parsley
- 1 teaspoon minced fresh basil leaves
- 1 teaspoon minced fresh tarragon leaves
- 1 teaspoon sugar
- ½ teaspoon freshly ground black pepper
- Pinch of salt

Combine all of the ingredients in a small mixing bowl. Adjust the seasoning with salt and pepper to taste before combining with the Cranberry Beans and Asparagus.

parma ham crisps

- ½ pound Parma ham (prosciutto may be substituted), sliced ¹⁄₁₆ inch thick

Preheat the oven to 450° F.

Place the ham slices flat on a baking sheet and cook in the oven until crisp, about 5 minutes. Remove from the oven and drain immediately on kitchen towels. While the ham is still warm, crumble into a bowl.

PINTO BEANS

Among the most popular beans in South America (where they originated) and the United States, especially the Southwest, pinto beans are closely related to kidney beans and are similarly shaped, though smaller. They are pinkish tan and dappled with brown flecks when raw (the color evens out when the beans are cooked) and, according to some food historians, are named after the pinto horse (pinto means "painted" in Spanish), which has a similarly mottled coat. Their flavor is earthy, and their texture mealy, and they are blessed with more fiber than any other legume. They are often used to make refried beans (boiled, mashed, then fried beans) and chili con carne. A new hybrid of the pinto bean is the rattlesnake bean, which is similar in appearance, though its shape is more square and blunt.

Pinto beans are sometimes referred to as red Mexican beans or Mexican strawberries (the name American cowboys bestowed upon them).

Pinto Beans with Parsley, Garlic, and Anchovy Dressing

IN THIS RECIPE PINTO BEANS are enhanced by the saltiness of the Parsley, Garlic, and Anchovy Dressing. This side dish works particularly well with grilled fish or shellfish.

Place the beans in a colander and pick over to remove any stones or discolored beans. Put the beans in a stockpot, cover with fresh cold water, and soak for at least 3 hours or preferably overnight to expedite the cooking process.

Drain the beans, return to a medium-sized, heavy stockpot, and cover with fresh water. Using the clove as a pin, attach the bay leaf to the whole onion. Add the studded onion and spices to the pot and bring to a rolling boil over high heat. Reduce the heat to a simmer and cook gently, uncovered, over medium-low heat until the beans are tender, about 45 minutes to 1 hour, skimming the surface from time to time to remove any scum that may have formed. Drain the beans, then return to the pot and cover to keep warm. Discard the onion, bay leaf, and clove.

- 1 cup dried pinto beans
- 1 clove
- 1 medium bay leaf
- 1 whole yellow onion, peeled
- Salt
- Freshly ground black pepper
- Parsley, Garlic, and Anchovy Dressing (recipe follows)

4 side dish servings

parsley, garlic, and anchovy dressing

- 1 large tomato, peeled, cored, seeded, and diced
- 8 canned anchovy fillets, rinsed with water, dried, and minced
- 6 cloves garlic, peeled and minced
- ½ cup minced fresh parsley leaves
- ½ teaspoon freshly ground black pepper
- 2 tablespoons champagne vinegar (apple cider vinegar or malt vinegar may be substituted)
- ¼ cup olive oil

Place all of the ingredients in a large mixing bowl and stir well to combine. Fold in the warm pinto beans and serve.

Scarlet Runner Beans with Crawfish and Ginger

SCARLET RUNNER BEANS

Scarlet runner beans grow on climbing vines with beautiful scarlet-orange flowers. The plant is so attractive that it was first brought to the British Isles from the Americas in the 17th century for ornamental purposes. The reddish beans are eaten fresh in their green pod and dried. Also edible are the flowers, which taste like the immature beans.

Scarlet runner beans are quite popular in England, Spain, Italy, and Holland. Also available are the related white runner beans.

IF DESIRED, THIS DISH CAN BE PRESENTED WARM (without marinating). I recommend that you serve it as a main course, perhaps with soft noodles or bulgur wheat.

- 1 cup dried scarlet runner beans
- 1 pound crawfish tails, boiled and peeled (cooked shrimp or crabmeat may be substituted)
- 1 pound unskinned yellow potatoes, boiled, then quartered
- 1 Vidalia onion, peeled and minced
- ½ cup dry sherry
- ¼ cup olive oil
- 2 tablespoons malt vinegar or any mild vinegar, such as champagne or apple cider vinegar
- ½ red bell pepper, cored, seeded, and finely diced
- ½ yellow bell pepper, cored, seeded, and finely diced
- ½ green bell pepper, cored, seeded, and finely diced
- 4 stalks celery, trimmed and finely diced
- 1 clove garlic, peeled and minced
- 1 tablespoon sugar
- 1 tablespoon finely minced, peeled, fresh ginger
- Salt to taste
- Freshly ground black pepper to taste

Place the beans in a heavy stockpot and cover with cold water. Bring to a boil, then reduce the heat to a simmer and cook, uncovered, for about 1 hour or until the beans are tender. Drain and allow to cool.

Combine all of the ingredients in a large mixing bowl and allow to marinate for 2 hours, stirring occasionally. Serve at room temperature.

4 to 6 main course servings

Fresh Butter Beans with Orange, Apple, and Roasted Garlic

LIMA BEANS

Lima beans are believed to have originated in the early sixteenth century in the high plains of Peru, and are named after Lima, the capital of that country. They boast a light buttery flavor and a creamy, starchy texture, and come in two sizes: The larger ones are called potato limas or butter, Madagascar, or Fordhook beans, and the smaller ones, which have thinner skin and are milder in flavor, are called baby limas. Both are pale green and plump, but they are not the same bean in a different stage of the life cycle; they are related to one another but do not belong to the same botanical classification.

A popular ingredient in the South, lima beans are served on their own as a side dish, in soups and salads, and in the Southern favorite, succotash (a combination of corn and lima beans introduced to New World colonists by Native Americans). Lima beans are also highlighted in the cuisines of South and Central America and Africa.

Fresh limas, usually in their dark green pods, are available in some markets during the summer; dried, canned, and frozen limas are available year-round. For an easy side dish, try briefly boiling the large limas, then tossing them with diced tomatoes and a little balsamic vinegar and brown sugar.

I ENJOY THE JUXTAPOSITION OF THE FLAVORS and textures in this appetizer: the refreshing citrus flavor of the oranges, the tartness and crispness of the Granny Smith apple, the creaminess of the butter beans, and the pungency of the roasted garlic. Be sure to combine these ingredients gently and at the last moment so that the fruit does not start to fall apart and the apple does not begin to brown.

- *2 cups shelled fresh butter (lima) beans*
- *1 cup orange juice*
- *1 tablespoon brown sugar*
- *1 teaspoon Roasted Garlic Purée (see page 181)*
- *2 large oranges, peeled and segmented*
- *1 large Granny Smith apple, peeled, cored, and finely grated*
- *1 tablespoon shredded fresh basil leaves*

Place the lima beans in a wide, shallow sauté pan large enough to accommodate the beans in a single layer. Add the orange juice, sugar, and garlic purée to the pan and bring to a boil over medium-high heat. Cook until 90 percent of the liquid has evaporated and the lima beans have a sugar-orange glaze.

Remove the pan from the heat and place the beans in a mixing bowl with the remaining ingredients. Divide among 6 plates and serve.

6 appetizer servings

Butter Beans and Braised Leeks

ALSO CALLED LIMA BEANS, these large beans take the name butter beans because they have a very buttery texture. They tend to be a little bland, so don't be afraid to season well. I like to serve this dish over steamed rice or chilled as a salad.

- 1 cup dried butter beans
- 2 tablespoons olive oil
- 1 large yellow onion, peeled and minced
- 2 cloves garlic, peeled and minced
- 1 medium bay leaf
- 6 pods cardamom, hulled and crushed
- 2 large leeks, thoroughly rinsed and white portions sliced into ½-inch rounds
- 1 large carrot, peeled and finely diced
- 1 cup dry white wine
- 2 medium tomatoes, peeled, cored, seeded, and diced
- 2 tablespoons champagne vinegar (malt vinegar or apple cider vinegar may be substituted)
- Salt to taste
- Freshly ground black pepper to taste

Place the butter beans in a heavy saucepan and cover with cold water. Bring to a boil over high heat, reduce to a simmer, and cook, covered (with the lid cracked), until the beans are tender, about 1 hour. Drain and cool.

Heat the olive oil in a large, heavy skillet over medium-high heat. Add the onions and garlic and sauté, stirring constantly, until soft, about 5 minutes. Add the bay leaf and cardamom and cook for 1 minute. Add the leek rounds and carrot, reduce the heat, and sauté, covered, for 5 minutes, stirring occasionally. Add the wine and tomatoes, bring to a simmer, then add the beans and cook for 5 minutes, uncovered, stirring constantly. Add the vinegar, salt, and pepper, stir well, and remove from the heat.

Serve hot or refrigerate until chilled.

4 appetizer or 2 main course servings

Baby Lima Beans
with Shrimp and Crawfish

THE DISH IS EXTREMELY POPULAR in the southern United States, where it is primarily made with shrimp and served over steamed rice. I decided to add crawfish to increase the textural variety. If fresh crawfish is unavailable, substitute crabmeat or double the quantity of shrimp.

Heat the oil in a small, heavy stockpot. Add the onion, garlic, and red pepper flakes, and sauté for 2 minutes. Add the shrimp and crawfish and sauté until just warmed through and the shrimp turn pink, about 30 seconds. Remove the seafood and vegetables from the pot, set aside in a bowl, and cover.

Place the beans, chicken stock, and bay leaf in the stockpot. Bring to a boil, then reduce the heat, cover, and simmer until the beans are tender, about 10 minutes for fresh beans and 45 minutes for dried, skimming the surface of the stock from time to time to remove any scum that may have formed.

Return the reserved seafood and vegetables to the pot, bring to a boil, reduce the heat, and simmer for 4 minutes to heat through. Season with salt and pepper.

Serve immediately with hot noodles or rice.

Note: Dried beans can be used in this recipe as long as they are soaked first: Place the beans in a mixing bowl and cover with cold water. Allow to soak for at least 3 hours or preferably overnight, then drain.

6 main course servings

- *2 tablespoons canola oil*
- *1 large yellow onion, peeled and finely diced*
- *2 large cloves garlic, peeled and minced*
- *Pinch of red pepper flakes*
- *1¼ pounds fresh peeled and deveined shrimp (21–25 shrimp per pound)*
- *1 pound fresh peeled crawfish tails*
- *1½ cups fresh baby lima beans (see Note)*
- *4 cups Chicken Stock (see page 181)*
- *1 medium bay leaf*
- *Salt to taste*
- *Freshly ground black pepper to taste*
- *Hot glass noodles, angel hair pasta, or rice, for serving*

FAVA BEANS

Fava beans, which can be traced back to Switzerland during the Bronze Age and have long been popular in many parts of Europe and the Middle East, are a relative newcomer to the American food scene. They can be eaten fresh and in the pod if picked when they are young and tender—in southern and central Italy, young, uncooked, fresh fava beans are dipped in coarse salt and eaten at the end of meals with Pecorino cheese—or shelled and peeled, or dried. Today in the United States fava beans are beginning to appear more often on menus, sometimes matched with such extravagant ingredients as lobster and truffles, sometimes prepared in a more rustic fashion, such as puréed for soups, sautéed with pancetta and onions, or tossed with linguine and olive oil.

Fresh favas have a wonderful sweet, nutty aroma and are preferable for most recipes; the dried beans have less flavor and tend to disintegrate if overcooked. When buying fresh favas (usually available only during a short period in late spring and early summer), look for small, young, pale green pods holding beans that are the same size as or marginally larger than butter beans. Dried fava beans can range in color from creamy beige to tan. Also available is a small, dark to greenish brown, Egyptian variety of fava called ful or fool, which is used to make the simmered dried bean dish called ful medames (or ful for short) that has been a mainstay in the Egyptian diet since ancient times.

Fava beans are also known as broad beans, Windsor beans, horse beans, and daffa beans.

Corn and Fava Bean Soup

I LIKE THE CONTRAST BETWEEN the smooth tomato and cucumber purée and the crisp uncooked vegetables in this chilled soup. The corn and favas add a note of earthiness to the flavor. Serve this soup with pita bread or grilled papadums.

- *1 cup fresh, shelled, skinned fava beans*
- *8 large tomatoes, peeled, cored, seeded, and finely chopped*
- *1 large cucumber, peeled, seeded, and finely chopped*
- *1 cup (2 ears) fresh corn kernels*
- *1 red onion, peeled and finely chopped*
- *½ red bell pepper, seeded and finely chopped*
- *½ yellow bell pepper, seeded and finely chopped*
- *½ green bell pepper, seeded and finely chopped*
- *2 stalks celery, trimmed and finely chopped*
- *2 cloves garlic, peeled and minced*
- *¼ cup olive oil*
- *¼ cup dry white wine*
- *1 tablespoon fresh lemon juice*
- *Dash of Pernod*
- *Salt to taste*
- *Freshly ground black pepper to taste*
- *1 large carrot, peeled and finely shredded, for garnish*

Place 3 cups water in a medium pot and bring to a boil over high heat. Add the fava beans, return to a boil, and cook for 3 minutes. Drain and allow the beans to cool.

Purée the tomatoes and cucumber together in a food processor set on high.

In a large soup tureen, combine the beans and the tomato and cucumber purée with the remaining ingredients, except the carrot. Chill. Garnish each portion with shredded carrot before serving.

6 to 8 appetizer servings

Fresh Baby Fava Beans with Shrimp and Sherry

I LIKE TO SERVE THIS DISH with the rice from Braised Basmati Rice with Lobster, Dried Tomatoes, and Yogurt Mint Sauce (see page 126). Follow the rice recipe as written, but omit the turmeric and lobster.

- 2 tablespoons olive oil
- ½ large yellow onion, peeled and finely chopped
- 1 large clove garlic, peeled and minced
- 1 medium bay leaf
- 1 large tomato, peeled, seeded, and diced
- 1 cup Chicken Stock (see page 181)
- ¼ cup dry sherry
- 4 cups fresh, shelled, skinned fava beans
- ¼ teaspoon salt
- ¼ teaspoon freshly ground black pepper
- 1 cup peeled, fresh, raw baby (small) shrimp
- Braised Basmati Rice (see above and page 126)

Heat the oil in a large, heavy saucepan over medium-high heat. Add the onion and garlic and sauté until translucent but not browned, about 2 minutes. Add the bay leaf and tomato and cook an additional 2 minutes.

Add the chicken stock and sherry and cook over high heat until reduced by half, about 5 minutes.

Add the fava beans, salt, and pepper, and cook for 1 minute over high heat. Stir in the shrimp, return the liquid to a boil, and cook the shrimp until they have turned pink and are heated through, about 1½ minutes.

Serve immediately with the Braised Basmati Rice described above.

6 main course servings

Haricots Verts with Poppy Seeds, Lemon, and Almonds

THIS DISH IS SIMPLY AN EXTENSION of haricots verts with almonds, a traditional French preparation.

- *1 pound fresh haricots verts (any fresh green bean may be substituted), washed and tough ends removed*
- *¼ cup sliced almonds*
- *1 tablespoon olive oil*
- *1 teaspoon poppy seeds*
- *¼ teaspoon red pepper flakes*
- *Juice of 1 lemon*
- *Salt to taste*
- *Freshly ground black pepper to taste*

Bring enough cold water to cover the haricots verts to a boil in a large sauté pan. Add the haricots verts and blanch for 3 minutes. Drain well.

Spread the almonds in a large sauté pan over low heat and toast gently, stirring constantly, until they turn a light golden brown. Add the oil, poppy seeds, red pepper flakes, and haricots verts, and sauté for 1 minute over medium-high heat, stirring to mix well. Remove from the heat. Add the lemon juice and salt and pepper. Serve.

4 to 6 appetizer servings

BLACK BEANS

Unlike other New World beans, such as navy and kidney beans, black beans never caught on in Europe. In Central and South America and the Caribbean, however, these matte black beans with cream-colored flesh, a sweet, earthy flavor, and a soft, mealy texture are a standard part of the diet. Feijoada—thinly sliced meats served with black beans and an assortment of other side dishes, including rice, kale or collard greens, orange slices and hot peppers—is the national dish of Brazil; fried black beans and rice, called gallo pinto, *is the national breakfast of Costa Rica; Cuba is known for its black bean soup and* moros y cristianos *(Moors and Christians, or black beans and white rice), and in Mexico black beans are incorporated into a wide assortment of dishes, including refried beans and bean burritos.*

Black beans are also known as turtle beans and frijoles negros.

SERVE THESE BEANS HOT with steamed rice or tortillas, or use them in Spinach and Bean Quesadillas (at right) or Black Bean Cakes with Potato Pepper Sauce (page 34). These beans also may be frozen in airtight containers for future use.

- *1 cup dried black beans*
- *1 large yellow onion, peeled and roughly chopped*
- *1 large green bell pepper, seeded and roughly chopped*
- *2 large cloves garlic, peeled and minced*
- *1 medium bay leaf*
- *1 teaspoon black pepper*
- *¼ teaspoon cumin*
- *¼ teaspoon coriander*
- *¼ teaspoon salt*
- *Pinch of cayenne pepper*

Place the beans in a colander and rinse with cold running water. Pick over the beans to remove any stones or foreign objects. Place the beans in a clean pot, cover with fresh cold water, and soak for at least 4 hours or preferably overnight to expedite the cooking process. Drain the beans.

In a large stainless steel pot, combine the beans, 1 quart water, and all of the remaining ingredients and bring to a boil. When the water reaches a boil, skim the surface, reduce the heat, and simmer until the beans are tender, about 1 hour. Drain the liquid from the beans and reserve for use in other recipes. Discard the bay leaf.

Makes 2¼ cups

Spinach and Black Bean Quesadillas

I LIKE TO CUT THESE LOWFAT QUESADILLAS into small wedges and serve them as appetizers or hors d'oeuvres. Or, for a light lunch, I leave them whole and accompany them with a crisp green salad dressed with the Potato-Pepper Sauce featured in the recipe for Black Bean Cakes (page 34).

Heat 1 tablespoon of the oil in a heavy nonstick skillet over medium-high heat. Add the onion, garlic, and jalapeño pepper, and sauté until soft, about 3 minutes. Add the mashed beans to the pan and sauté for 1 minute. Fold in the spinach, stirring well to incorporate. Remove the pan from the heat and allow the mixture to cool. Season with the five-spice powder and salt and pepper.

Place 6 of the tortillas flat on a work surface and divide the bean mixture among them, spreading the filling on top of each tortilla but leaving a $\frac{1}{2}$-inch border around the tortilla edges. Brush the tortilla edges with beaten egg, then place a second tortilla on top, pressing down to seal.

Preheat the oven to 200° F.

Place a heavy skillet over medium-high heat. Brush the tops and bottoms of the tortillas with the remaining oil and cook each one in the hot skillet until light brown, about 2 minutes on each side. Keep the finished quesadillas warm in the preheated oven until all of them are cooked.

Remove the quesadillas from the oven. Leave whole or cut into wedges and serve immediately.

12 appetizer or 6 main course servings

- *3 tablespoons olive oil*
- *$\frac{1}{2}$ cup chopped yellow onion*
- *2 cloves garlic, peeled and minced*
- *1 jalapeño pepper, stemmed, seeded, and minced*
- *1 cup cooked Black Beans, mashed (at left)*
- *1 cup cooked spinach, excess water squeezed out*
- *Pinch of five-spice powder (available at Asian or other specialty food stores)*
- *Salt to taste*
- *Freshly ground black pepper to taste*
- *12 (8-inch) soft whole-wheat tortillas*
- *1 egg, well beaten*

Black Bean Cakes
with Potato-Pepper Sauce

FOR VARIETY, top these cakes with poached eggs or grilled shrimp or chicken along with the sauce.

> • 2¼ cups cooked Black Beans (see page 32)
> • 2 tablespoons olive oil
> • Potato-Pepper Sauce (recipe follows)

Divide the cooked beans into 2 equal parts. Place one portion in a heavy saucepan and add ½ cup reserved cooking liquid. Cook over medium heat until the beans can be mashed into a paste with a fork, about 30 minutes; if necessary, add additional liquid while cooking to achieve this consistency.

Drain the beans, reserving the cooking liquid, and place in a large mixing bowl. Mash the beans with a fork or hand mixer until they reach the consistency of mashed potatoes. If the mixture is too thick, dilute slightly with some of the reserved bean cooking liquid. Blend in the reserved portion of beans with a wooden spoon and allow the mixture to cool.

Using a round cookie cutter, form the bean mixture into individual cakes, approximately 3 inches in diameter and 1 inch high.

Heat the olive oil in a large sauté pan over medium heat. Add 2 bean cakes at a time and gently sauté on both sides, cooking for about 1 minute on each side. Place 2 cakes on each serving plate and garnish with Potato-Pepper Sauce.

4 appetizer servings

potato-pepper sauce

POTATOES BAKED on top of a layer of salt, as in this recipe, are much fluffier than potatoes baked in any other way. In addition to serving this sauce with Black Bean Cakes, I like to use it as a virtually fat-free substitute for mayonnaise.

- 2 large baking potatoes
- 1 pound kosher or sea salt
- 1 jalapeño pepper, seeded and finely diced
- 1 tablespoon fresh cilantro leaves, finely chopped
- 2 tablespoons sour cream
- 1 tablespoon rice wine vinegar
- 1 tablespoon ketchup
- Approximately ½ cup reserved cooking liquid from Black Bean Cakes (if necessary to thin sauce)

Preheat the oven to 425° F.

Wash and dry the potatoes. Spread the salt evenly on a baking sheet. Place the potatoes on the salt and bake for approximately 45 minutes. Remove the potatoes from the oven and dust off any salt that is sticking to the skins.

Place the remaining ingredients except the reserved cooking liquid in the bowl of a food processor. Split the potatoes lengthwise and, with a spoon, scoop out the flesh and place in the processor. Blend on high speed for 45 seconds. If the sauce is too thick, dilute to desired consistency with the reserved bean cooking liquid. (The consistency of the sauce should range between mayonnaise and cream.) Serve with Black Bean Cakes.

NAVY BEANS

Indigenous to the New World, navy beans are mild, mealy, and white. They are about ¼ inch long and oval, and are sometimes confused with pea beans (which are about half the size) and Great Northern beans (which are about twice the size, less plump, and more kidneylike in shape). Fortunately, these three types of white beans can be used interchangeably.

Fed to sailors on United States ships since the mid-1800s, hence their name, navy beans are commonly used to make soups, stews, and casseroles as well as Boston baked beans (though many New Englanders prefer to use pea beans instead of navy beans for this classic regional dish).

Navy beans are sometimes referred to as Yankee or Boston beans.

Navy Beans

SERVE THESE BEANS HOT over steamed rice or use in Brandade of Navy Beans (page 42) or Navy Bean and Onion Soup (at right).

> · 1 cup dried navy beans
> · 2 tablespoons virgin olive oil
> · 1 large onion, peeled and finely diced
> · 2 cloves garlic, peeled and minced
> · 1 medium bay leaf
> · 1 sprig fresh thyme
> · 4 cups Chicken Stock (see page 181)
> · Salt to taste
> · Freshly ground black pepper to taste

Place the beans in a colander and rinse with cold running water. Pick over the beans to remove any stones or foreign objects.

Heat the oil over medium-high heat in a large, heavy stockpot. Add the onion and garlic and sauté for 5 minutes or until the onion becomes transparent. Add the bay leaf and thyme and sauté for 1 minute. Add the beans and chicken stock and bring to a boil over high heat. Reduce the heat, cover, and simmer for 45 minutes or until the beans are tender. Uncover the pot and skim the surface of the bean liquid from time to time to remove any scum that may have formed.

Remove the pot from the heat, season the beans with salt and pepper to taste, and drain any excess liquid from the beans. Remove the bay leaf and serve hot.

Makes 2½ cups

Navy Bean and Onion Soup

THIS SOUP IS EXTREMELY HEARTY and makes an ample main course, particularly on a cold winter night.

> · 2 tablespoons olive oil
> · 3 large yellow onions, peeled and thinly sliced
> · 4 cloves garlic, peeled and minced
> · 8 French shallots, peeled and thinly sliced
> · 1 medium bay leaf
> · Pinch of fresh thyme
> · Pinch of fresh rosemary
> · 2 cups cooked Navy Beans (at left)
> · 1 cup dry white wine
> · 1 cup Madeira
> · 1 quart Chicken Stock (see page 181) or Vegetable Stock (see page 180), plus extra if needed to thin the soup
> · Salt to taste
> · Freshly ground black pepper to taste
> · 4 to 6 tablespoons crumbled Roquefort cheese

Heat the oil in a heavy stockpot over medium-high heat. Add the onion, garlic, and shallots, and quickly sauté until golden brown, stirring continuously. Add the bay leaf, thyme, and rosemary, and sauté for 1 minute. Add the beans, wine, and Madeira, stirring well. Add the stock, stirring to incorporate the ingredients, and bring to a boil. Reduce the heat, cover, and simmer for 45 minutes, stirring occasionally. (The longer the beans cook the more they will fall apart and thicken the soup. If a smoother, creamier consistency is desired, remove the pot from the stove and purée the soup in the pot with a hand blender. If the soup appears too thick, dilute it with stock until the desired consistency is reached.)

Remove the pot from the heat and adjust the seasonings to taste. Ladle the soup into cups and sprinkle each with a tablespoon of the cheese.

4 to 6 main course servings

French Navy Bean and Arugula Salad with Seared Anise Tuna

HERE I USE NAVY BEANS IN TWO WAYS: whole with the arugula in the salad and puréed with the remaining ingredients in the salad dressing. The meaty texture and distinct flavor of the Seared Anise Tuna combine beautifully with the sharpness of the arugula and the creaminess of the dressing.

Place the beans in a heavy stockpot and cover with cold water. Bring to a boil, then reduce heat to a simmer and cook, uncovered, for 30 minutes or until the beans are tender. Drain and allow to cool.

- 1 cup dried navy beans
- ¼ cup olive oil
- 1 teaspoon freshly ground black pepper
- ½ red onion, peeled and minced
- 1 large tomato, peeled, seeded, cored, and diced
- Pinch of nutmeg
- Juice of 1 lemon
- 2 tablespoons champagne vinegar (malt or apple cider vinegar may be substituted)
- 1 teaspoon sugar
- 2 tablespoons dry sherry
- 1 teaspoon chili powder
- Salt to taste
- 8 cups washed and dried arugula
- Seared Anise Tuna (recipe follows)

Divide the beans into two equal portions. Place one portion in a food processor with the remaining ingredients through the salt and blend on high for 1 minute, until the mixture is the consistency of heavy cream. If it appears too thick, dilute the dressing with a little water.

Toss the remaining beans with the arugula in a large salad bowl, then drizzle with the puréed bean dressing. Serve at room temperature with Seared Anise Tuna. Any remaining dressing can be refrigerated for up to 6 days.

4 main course servings

seared anise tuna

In a small bowl, grind the anise and salt together to form a powder, then mix in the oil. Brush the anise mixture evenly over the tuna slices.

- 6 pods star anise
- Pinch of salt
- 2 tablespoons canola oil
- 8 2-ounce slices fresh tuna

Heat a heavy skillet over high heat. Add the oiled tuna slices and sear for 30 seconds on each side. Remove and serve with the French Navy Bean and Arugula Salad.

Cassoulet of Navy Beans and Smoked Chicken with Jalapeño Corn Bread

THIS IS A HEALTHY VARIATION on the traditional French cassoulet, which is usually made with high-fat sausages, bacon, and ham. As this is an American version, I serve it with Jalapeño Corn Bread.

Place the beans in a colander and pick over to remove any stones or discolored beans. Rinse the beans under cold running water, then place in a stockpot, cover with fresh cold water, and soak for at least 3 hours or preferably overnight to expedite the cooking process.

- *1 pound dried navy beans*
- *1 whole 3-pound smoked chicken*
- *1 large yellow onion, peeled and diced*
- *4 large cloves garlic, peeled and minced*
- *¼ teaspoon minced fresh thyme*
- *Pinch of cayenne pepper*
- *1 medium bay leaf*
- *4 cups Chicken Stock (see page 181)*
- *½ teaspoon salt*
- *½ teaspoon freshly ground black pepper*
- *¼ cup fresh bread crumbs*
- *Jalapeño Corn Bread (recipe follows)*

Place the chicken on a large cutting board. Pull off the legs, remove the skin, and pick the meat from the bones. Reserve the bones and skin. Carefully remove the skin from the rest of the chicken and place with the leg bones and skin. With a sharp knife, make a cut down the length of the breast on both sides of the breast bone. Remove the meat by pulling backward from the wishbone. Place the white meat from the carcass with the leg meat and set aside.

Return the chicken carcass, skin, and leg bones to the cutting board and, with a heavy knife or cleaver, chop everything into pieces measuring about 1 inch.

Place the bone and skin pieces in a medium-sized, heavy stockpot, add 2 cups water, and simmer over low heat until all the water is gone and the fat has been rendered. (You will be left with a milky, fatty liquid.) Keep cooking this liquid until it becomes clear. Remove the pan from the heat and strain the liquid through a fine sieve into a clean bowl. Discard the bones and skin.

Return 4 tablespoons of the rendered fat to the dirty pot. (Do not concern yourself with the residue remaining in the base of the pot. It contains a lot of flavor, as does the rendered chicken fat.)

Drain the soaked beans. Add the onion, garlic, thyme, cayenne pepper, and bay leaf to the stockpot with the fat and sauté over medium heat for 3 minutes or until the onion is transparent but not browned. Add the beans and chicken stock to the pot and bring to a boil over high heat, skimming any fat or scum that may rise to the surface. Reduce the heat to a simmer and cook slowly, uncovered, until the beans are soft, about 2 hours.

Preheat the oven to 300° F.

Add the reserved chicken meat and the salt and black pepper to the pot, stirring well. Ladle the bean-chicken mixture into a large ovenproof dish and sprinkle with the bread crumbs. Bake slowly for 1 to 1½ hours, until the top crust is golden brown. Serve hot in individual bowls with Jalapeño Corn Bread.

6 main course servings

jalapeño corn bread

I PREFER TO COOK corn bread in a cast-iron skillet because it conducts heat more evenly than an ordinary baking pan and thus yields a better-textured bread.

Preheat the oven to 375° F.

In a mixing bowl, combine the cornmeal and salt. Combine the butter, water, and jalapeño pepper in a small saucepan and bring to a boil. Remove from the heat. Add ¼ cup of the water mixture to the cornmeal. Add the baking soda and mix to a paste. Allow the cornmeal to swell, then add the remaining water mixture, stirring well.

Pour the batter into a greased 9-inch round baking pan or cast-iron skillet and bake for 35 to 40 minutes or until golden brown. Remove from the oven and allow to rest for 10 minutes. Cut the corn bread into wedges and serve with Cassoulet of Navy Beans and Smoked Chicken.

- *2 cups yellow cornmeal*
- *¼ teaspoon salt*
- *2 tablespoons unsalted butter*
- *1 cup water*
- *1 large jalapeño pepper, seeded and minced*
- *½ teaspoon baking soda*

Brandade of Navy Beans

IN THE CLASSIC BRANDADE RECIPE FROM PROVENCE, salt cod, olive oil, garlic, and milk are pounded together, then served as a dip. In my version white beans replace the salt cod, and the mixture is combined in a food processor.

Place the beans in a colander and pick over to remove any stones or discolored beans. Place the beans in a heavy stockpot, cover with fresh cold water, and soak for at least 3 hours or preferably overnight to expedite the cooking process.

- *1½ cups dried navy beans*
- *1 medium bay leaf*
- *1 sprig fresh thyme*
- *1 sprig fresh rosemary*
- *1 pint Chicken Stock (see page 181)*
- *4 cloves garlic, crushed*
- *¾ cup extra-virgin olive oil*
- *Juice of 1 lemon*
- *¼ cup heavy cream*
- *Salt to taste*
- *Freshly ground black pepper to taste*
- *Toasted pita or French bread or crudités, for serving*

Drain the beans and return to the stockpot.

Place the bay leaf, thyme, and rosemary in the center of a 4-inch square of cheesecloth, then tie the ends of the cloth in a knot to form a sachet.

Add the chicken stock and sachet to the beans. Bring to a boil, reduce the heat, cover, and simmer until the beans are tender but not mushy, approximately 35 to 40 minutes. Uncover and skim the surface of the stock from time to time to remove any scum that may have formed.

Remove the pot from the heat and discard the sachet. Place the beans in a food processor with the garlic and olive oil, and blend. Slowly add the lemon juice and cream, blending until well incorporated but not over-mixed. Season with salt and pepper, then pour into a bowl. Serve with toasted pita or French bread or crudités.

4 appetizer servings

Five-Bean Salad with Truffle Oil Dressing and Rosemary Grilled Quail

I KNOW THAT THIS RECIPE might seem an incredible amount of work, but I promise the flavors of the salad make the effort worthwhile. It is difficult to suggest an alternative for truffled olive oil (sold at specialty food stores), as the flavor is so distinct; however, if you must, use an extremely high-quality, extra-virgin olive oil.

This bean salad is excellent as a complete meal, or it can be served as an accompaniment to any grilled or roasted meat. I particularly like it with Rosemary Grilled Quail (recipe follows).

- *½ cup dried cranberry beans, covered in water and soaked for at least 2 hours*
- *½ cup dried corona beans, covered in water and soaked for at least 2 hours*
- *½ cup dried pavom (rattlesnake) beans, covered in water and soaked for at least 2 hours*
- *½ cup dried flageolet beans (pale green kidney beans)*
- *½ cup dried navy beans*
- *Truffle Oil Dressing (recipe follows)*
- *Rosemary Grilled Quail (recipe follows)*

sachets

- *5 sprigs fresh thyme*
- *1 pound smoked bacon, diced*
- *5 medium bay leaves*
- *10 cloves garlic, peeled*
- *2½ gallons Chicken Stock (see page 181)*

For each type of bean, pour 1 quart chicken stock into a large saucepan. Add the respective bean variety and 1 sachet. Bring the stock to a boil, lower the heat, cover, and simmer until tender, using the following list of cooking times as a guide:

Cranberry: approximately 1½ to 2 hours

Corona: approximately 1½ to 2 hours

Pavom: approximately 1½ to 2 hours

Flageolet: approximately 45 minutes to 1 hour

Navy: approximately 45 minutes to 1 hour

The beans in this recipe are cooked in 5 separate batches and cooking times vary to ensure that all types are cooked evenly; the beans cannot be cooked together. Five sachets will need to be made to flavor the beans while cooking: Cut 5 muslin squares to measure approximately 4" x 4" each. Into each place 1 sprig thyme, one-fifth of the diced bacon, 1 bay leaf, and 2 cloves garlic. Pull the corners of the muslin together to form a purse and tie with string.

Uncover and skim the surface of the stock from time to time to remove any scum that may have formed.

Drain the beans as they become tender, discarding the stock and sachets, and allow to cool.

Fold the cooled beans into the Truffle Oil Dressing. Serve with the Rosemary Grilled Quail.

truffle oil dressing

- 1 large red onion, peeled and finely diced
- 1 medium carrot, peeled and finely diced
- 1 large tomato, peeled, cored, seeded, and finely diced
- ½ cup truffled olive oil
- ½ cup dry sherry
- ¼ cup sherry vinegar
- ¼ cup sugar
- ¼ cup minced fresh flat-leaf parsley
- 1 tablespoon fresh shredded basil leaves
- ½ teaspoon fresh thyme, minced
- 1 teaspoon dry mustard powder
- 1 teaspoon freshly ground black pepper
- ½ teaspoon white pepper
- Salt to taste

While the last of the beans are cooling, combine all of the ingredients for the dressing in a mixing bowl.

rosemary grilled quail

- 8 strong rosemary branches
- 16 deboned quail
- 2 tablespoons virgin olive oil
- Salt
- Freshly ground black pepper

Preheat a grill or broiler.

Remove the leaves from the bottom half of the rosemary branches, then sharpen the ends with a knife to make points. Set aside.

Rub the quails lightly with the olive oil, then season lightly with salt and pepper. Carefully thread 2 quail on each rosemary skewer and cook on a hot grill or in a broiler for 3 minutes on each side.

Place the quails on serving plates with the Five-Bean Salad.

16 appetizer or 8 main course servings

SOYBEANS

Soybeans and products made from them, such as tofu, have been an important source of protein in the Asian diet for thousands of years. Americans have until recently valued soybeans more as an export crop, animal feed, and industrial commodity (used to make such products as plastic, paint, and soap). However, with the trend in the United States toward lowering meat consumption and the increasing interest in Asian cuisines, soybeans and soybean products have begun to gain in popularity as a food source.

There are more than 1,000 soybean varieties; the ones most common in the United States are tan or black (with a tan interior) and pea-sized. While soybeans can be eaten either fresh or dried or even roasted like peanuts, many people consider their flavor rather bland and, in the case of the dried beans, do not want to bother with the long cooking time required. Many soybean-based products, on the other hand, are easy to cook with and add exciting flavor and texture to our diets. Among them: soy sauce (made from fermented soybeans paired with a roasted grain such as wheat or barley); tamari (a wheat-free soy sauce); miso (fermented soybean paste); tofu (a custard-like cake made by curdling soy milk—which on its own is an easily digestible alternative for lactose-intolerant people); and tempeh (fermented soybean cake). Other soybean products include soy flour, which boasts twice the protein of wheat flour and is used in many meat substitutes as well in baking (often combined with wheat flour), and soybean sprouts, which, unlike mung bean sprouts (the kind of sprouts most commonly found in U.S. markets), need to be blanched or cooked before eating.

Soybeans are also known as soya beans and soy peas.

Tofu with Napa Cabbage

TOFU, WHICH IS rather tasteless on its own, has the terrific ability to absorb the flavors with which it is combined, making it a great addition to vegetable stir-fries and soups. If possible, buy tofu loose from a tub (rather than prepackaged), giving it a good sniff to check its freshness; there is hardly anything that tastes quite so bad as sour tofu. Before preparing tofu, rinse it in cold water for a few minutes to remove any residue.

- *1 tablespoon cumin*
- *1 tablespoon coriander*
- *1 teaspoon poppy seeds*
- *½ teaspoon dried lemon peel*
- *½ teaspoon freshly ground black pepper*
- *Pinch of cayenne pepper*
- *Pinch of white pepper*
- *2 cups firm, fresh tofu, cut into ½-inch dice*
- *2 tablespoons canola oil*
- *3 cups shredded Napa cabbage (bok choy, broccoli rabe, or any other leafy vegetable may be substituted)*
- *1 clove garlic, peeled and minced*

In a shallow dish, mix together the cumin, coriander, poppy seeds, dried lemon peel, and black, cayenne, and white pepper. Dry the tofu pieces on kitchen towels and gently roll in the dried ingredients so that the seasoning adheres and forms a coating.

Heat the oil over medium heat in a large, heavy sauté pan. Add the tofu and gently sauté for about 2 minutes, stirring occasionally. Remove the tofu to a plate, cover, and keep warm.

Return the pan to the heat, add the cabbage and garlic, and sauté quickly over high heat until the cabbage is wilted, about 2 minutes.

Divide the cabbage among 4 plates, top with the sautéed tofu, and serve immediately.

4 appetizer servings

Grilled Pheasant Breasts with Miso Sauce or Tamari Dipping Sauce

grilled pheasant breasts

I PRESENT TWO DIFFERENT sauce choices for the grilled pheasant: The Miso Sauce is more complex in flavor and is meant to be spooned over the pheasant. The slightly sweet Tamari Dipping Sauce is served on the side and, as its name suggests, is meant for dipping.

- 6 boneless pheasant breasts (see Note)
- 4 egg whites
- 1 tablespoon freshly ground black pepper
- Pinch of salt
- 1 small clove garlic, peeled and minced
- 1 tablespoon minced fresh cilantro leaves
- 1 teaspoon lemon juice
- 2 tablespoons peanut oil
- 1 teaspoon toasted sesame seeds
- Miso Sauce or Tamari Dipping Sauce (recipes follow)

Place the pheasant breasts in a mixing bowl, cover with the egg whites, and marinate for about 1 hour. (This process will plump up the breasts so that they will not dry out during cooking.)

In a small bowl, combine the pepper, salt, garlic, cilantro, lemon juice, and 1 tablespoon of the oil and mix to a paste. Remove the breasts from the egg whites, rinse under cold running water, and pat dry on kitchen towels. Brush each breast with the paste on the side of the breast that was attached to the carcass. Set in a clean dish.

Bring a grill or griddle up to a high temperature (coals on a grill should be grayish white and a griddle should be just below smoking). Brush each breast with a small amount of the remaining paste, then place on the grill or griddle, seasoned side down. Cook slowly for about 5 minutes, then turn and cook an additional 5 minutes on the second side. Remove the breasts from the grill, sprinkle with the sesame seeds, and serve hot with either Miso Sauce or Tamari Dipping Sauce.

Note: If possible, use wild instead of farmed pheasant for this recipe. Or, if pheasant is unavailable, substitute chicken, partridge, or quail.

6 main course servings

miso sauce

In a small dish, mix the arrowroot and vinegar into a loose paste. Set aside.

Heat the oil in a large, heavy saucepan over medium-high heat. Add the garlic and sauté for 1 minute or until just softened but not browned. Add the miso paste and stir. Add the chicken stock and bring to a simmer. Fold in the tamari

- 1 tablespoon arrowroot
- 2 tablespoons rice wine vinegar
- 1 tablespoon peanut oil
- 2 cloves garlic, peeled and minced
- 1 cup red (aka) miso paste (available at Japanese food stores)
- 3 cups Chicken Stock (see page 181)
- 1 teaspoon tamari
- 4 scallions, whites and greens, finely minced
- ¼ cup firm tofu, cut into ¼-inch cubes
- Pinch of red pepper flakes

and scallions and stir well. Gradually stir the arrowroot paste into the simmering stock until the stock is thick enough to coat the back of a spoon (it may not be necessary to add all of the arrowroot paste). Remove the pan from the heat and fold in the tofu and red pepper flakes. Cover and keep warm until ready to serve.

tamari dipping sauce

THIS ALTERNATIVE SAUCE for the grilled pheasants is also good served over hot or cold buckwheat noodles.

- 1 pint sake
- 1 cup tamari
- 1 pound sugar

Combine all of the ingredients in a heavy saucepan and reduce over medium heat until the sauce coats the back of a spoon. Remove from the heat and allow to cool slightly. Serve with the Grilled Pheasant Breasts.

Poached Chicken with Miso Sauce

Miso (fermented soybean paste) is made in a variety of colors and textures. My favorite, especially with poultry, is red miso (called *aka miso* in Japan), which has a bitter, fermented flavor.

Red miso is available in most Japanese grocery stores. If you cannot find it, choose another kind of miso as long as it has no additives, such as MSG. Note that miso is quite acidic and high in sodium and should be used sparingly.

Lay the chicken pieces on the bottom of a heavy 4-quart saucepan and cover by 1 inch with cold water. Add the onion, ginger, garlic, bay leaf, and star anise to the pan and bring to a boil. Skim the surface, cover, reduce the heat, and simmer for 45 minutes. Remove the chicken pieces to a plate and cover to keep warm.

Strain the cooking liquid into a clean saucepan, return to low heat, and gently stir in the miso paste. When the paste is incorporated, add the mushrooms and bring to a simmer. Add the rice noodles and simmer for an additional 5 minutes. Return the chicken pieces to the pan and stir in the sherry. Sprinkle in the scallions, cilantro, and red pepper flakes. Divide among 4 bowls. Garnish each serving with lemon zest.

4 main course servings

- 1 2- to 3-pound whole chicken, skinned and cut into 4 pieces (2 breasts and 2 legs)
- 1 large yellow onion, peeled and finely diced
- 1 tablespoon minced fresh gingerroot
- 2 cloves garlic, peeled and minced
- 1 bay leaf
- 2 pods star anise
- 1 cup red (aka) miso paste (available at Japanese food stores)
- 10 shiitake mushrooms, stems discarded, finely sliced
- 2 ounces rice noodles
- ½ cup dry sherry
- 6 scallions, both greens and whites, finely minced
- 1 tablespoon minced fresh cilantro leaves
- Pinch of red pepper flakes
- 1 teaspoon fresh lemon zest, for garnish

Mung Bean Sprout Salad with Shrimp, Rice Wine Vinegar, and Papaya

MUNG BEANS

Mung beans are best known in the United States in the form of bean sprouts. In other countries their uses are more diverse. In northern India, where they were first cultivated around 1500 B.C., these ¼-inch round beans (which can range in color from green to brown to black) are a dietary staple used to make dals (cooked, often puréed beans, peas, or lentils) as well as batters. In many Asian cuisines mung bean flour is used to make desserts, and the starch from the flour is mixed with water to make noodles known by various names, including saifun (in Japan), bean thread vermicelli, cellophane noodles, and pea starch noodles.

When mung beans are sprouted they become easier to digest because the starches in the beans are transformed into simple sugars. Contrary to popular belief, mung bean sprouts (and sprouts in general) are not nutritional powerhouses, though they are a wholesome, healthy addition to a diet.

IN THIS RECIPE, soft, sweet papaya provides a refreshing contrast to the crunchy texture of the mung beans and the sour flavor of the rice wine vinegar.

- ⅓ cup rice wine vinegar
- ¼ cup sesame oil
- 1 stalk lemon grass, finely chopped (available in Asian or other specialty food stores)
- 1 tablespoon honey
- 1 teaspoon soy sauce
- 1 teaspoon red (aka) miso paste (available in Japanese food stores)
- 1 clove garlic, peeled and minced
- Pinch of black pepper
- 4 cups mung bean sprouts
- 1 fresh papaya, peeled, seeded, and finely diced
- 1 cup cooked and peeled baby (small) shrimp

Place all of the ingredients except the sprouts, papaya, and shrimp in a large, heavy saucepan. Bring the mixture to a simmer over medium heat and cook for 2 minutes. Remove the pan from the heat and allow to stand for 2 hours.

Strain the sauce into a large bowl. Add the sprouts, papaya, and shrimp to the bowl and toss until well coated with the sauce. Serve.

4 salad servings

Mung Bean Salad with Star Anise, Garlic, and Lime

WHILE THE CARAMELIZED sugar adds depth and the star anise fruitiness, it is the lime that contributes the acidity needed to pull this salad together. Do not shred the Belgian endive until the last moment as it will oxidize very quickly.

Place the beans in a colander and pick over to remove any stones or foreign objects. Rinse the beans under cold running water, then place in a clean pot and cover with fresh cold water. Allow to soak for at least 4 hours or preferably overnight to expedite the cooking process. Drain the beans.

In a large, heavy pot, cover the beans with cold water and bring to a boil. Skim the surface when the water reaches a boil. Cover and cook for approximately 1 hour or until the beans are tender, skimming the surface occasionally to remove any scum that may have formed. Drain into a colander and rinse under cold running water to cool.

Cook the sugar, stirring constantly, in a heavy skillet over low heat until it dissolves and caramelizes, about 3 minutes. Add the star anise and lime juice and stir until the sugar completely dissolves. Remove from the heat.

Place the mung beans in a large bowl. Add the caramel mixture, then the oil, scallions, and red pepper flakes. Stir well and allow to cool to room temperature. Remove the star anise. Serve the beans on the shredded endive.

4 salad servings

- *1 cup dried mung beans*
- *2 tablespoons sugar*
- *4 pods star anise*
- *Juice of 1 lime*
- *2 tablespoons canola oil*
- *2 scallions, greens and whites, minced*
- *Pinch of red pepper flakes*
- *4 heads Belgian endive, ends discarded and shredded*

Lentils and Peas

LENTILS

PAGE 54

Clockwise from top:

brown lentils,

red/pink lentils,

green lentils,

green split peas,

yellow split peas

PAGE 55

Clockwise from top right:

black-eyed peas,

chick-peas,

fresh green peas

Lentils, tiny disk-shaped legumes, grow in pods on a climbing vine similar to the pea. Though their origin is unknown, it is hypothesized that they date back about 8,000 years and originated somewhere around present-day Iraq or Turkey. They are known to have played an important role in the diets of the ancient Greeks, Romans, Egyptians, and Hebrews, and today are most widely consumed in India, the Middle East, and Africa; lentils are also a frequent ingredient in soups in many parts of Europe. In India, lentils (often skinned and split in half) are served with nearly every meal, and are also ground into flour.

These wonderful little "lenses," which is what the word lentil means in Latin, come in numerous colors, ranging from russet brown to olive green to orangey-red to yellow to black. The most expensive of all lentils are French green lentils or lentilles du Puy, *which are a dark brownish green on the outside and yellow on the inside; they are firmer than most other lentils and boast a slightly peppery flavor. Packaged French green lentils also tend to be very consistent in size and quality.*

Lentils do not need to be presoaked, and they cook quickly. Lentils that hold their shape after cooking, such as brown or green lentils, are best in salads. Lentils that soften quickly (e.g., red lentils) work well in purées and as a thickening agent for soups and salad dressings (for best results, purée the lentils before adding them to the liquid to be thickened). Lentils sold in the United States as dhal *(the word used for lentils in India) have been skinned and are much lower in dietary fiber than unskinned lentils.*

Spiced Lentils with Apple Crisps and Curried Yogurt

In a large, heavy saucepan, heat the oil over medium-high heat. Add the onion and sauté until soft, about 4 minutes. Add the garam masala, bay leaf, and apples, and cook, stirring continuously, for 2 more minutes. Add the lentils and stock and bring the mixture to a boil over high heat. Reduce to a simmer and cook for about 25 minutes or until the lentils are tender, being careful not to overcook them. Remove the pan from the heat, remove the bay leaf, and adjust seasoning to taste.

Serve the lentils hot in one large serving bowl. Serve the yogurt and apple crisps separately and invite diners to combine all three components to their personal taste.

- 1 tablespoon canola oil
- 1 large yellow onion, peeled and finely diced
- 1 teaspoon garam masala (Indian spice mixture sold at Indian and other specialty food stores)
- 1 medium bay leaf
- 2 Granny Smith apples, peeled, cored, and finely diced
- 1 cup dried green lentils
- 2 cups Chicken Stock (see page 181)
- Apple Crisps (recipe follows)
- Curried Yogurt (recipe follows)

4 appetizer or 2 main course servings

apple crisps

LEFTOVER apple crisps make a delicious snack.

Preheat the oven to its lowest setting.

- 1 tablespoon confectioner's sugar
- Juice of 2 lemons
- 2 Granny Smith apples, peeled and cored

In a small bowl, dissolve the sugar in the lemon juice. Thinly slice the apples horizontally into rounds approximately 1/16 inch thick. Lay the apple slices on a baking sheet lined with parchment paper and brush lightly with the sugared lemon juice. Place the baking sheet in the oven and allow the apples to dry, about 3 to 4 hours or overnight.

Remove the baking sheet from the oven and gently peel the apple slices from the paper. (Some discoloration of the apple slices will occur.) Store in an airtight container until ready to use. They will last for 2 days in the refrigerator.

curried yogurt

Heat a small nonstick skillet over medium heat. Add the curry powder and toast until you can smell its intense aroma, about 30 seconds. Remove pan from heat.

- 1 tablespoon curry powder or garam masala (Indian spice mixture sold at Indian and other specialty food stores)
- 1 banana, peeled and finely diced
- 2 cups plain yogurt

Combine the curry powder with the banana and yogurt in a serving bowl, stirring well. Refrigerate until ready to use.

Makes 2 cups

Pink Lentils
with Iced Beet Tea

To scoop up the lentils, I suggest you serve *papadums,* the unleavened, wafer-shaped Indian bread made with lentil flour. *Papadums,* plain or seasoned with garlic or pepper, can be purchased at specialty food stores. Before serving they should be fried in oil, grilled, or baked in the oven until crisp. If *papadums* are unavailable, substitute *lavasch* or pita bread.

- *1½ cups pink lentils*
- *2 tablespoons peanut or vegetable oil*
- *1 large carrot, peeled and finely diced*
- *1 large yellow onion, peeled and finely diced*
- *2 tablespoons peeled and finely chopped gingerroot*
- *1 large clove garlic, peeled and minced*
- *1 medium bay leaf*
- *1 teaspoon garam masala (Indian spice mixture)*
- *5 cups Chicken Stock (see page 181) or water*
- *½ cup chopped fresh cilantro leaves*
- *¼ teaspoon freshly ground black pepper*
- *Salt to taste*
- *Beet Tea (recipe follows)*
- *8 papadums*

Place the lentils in a colander and pick over to remove any stones or foreign objects. Rinse under cold running water until the water runs clear. Drain.

Heat the oil in a heavy stockpot. Add the carrot, onion, ginger, garlic, bay leaf, and garam masala, and sauté over low heat for 5 minutes or until soft. Add the lentils and chicken stock to the pot and bring to a boil. Reduce the heat to a simmer, cover, and cook for 20 to 25 minutes or until the lentils are tender throughout but still hold their shape. Remove the pot from the heat and keep warm. Just prior to serving, add the cilantro, pepper, and salt to taste. Serve with Beet Tea and papadums.

4 appetizer or 2 main course servings

iced beet tea

MOST PEOPLE are surprised (happily so) by the natural sweetness of beet tea. Show off its bright magenta color in a clear glass.

> • 1 quart water
> • 4 large beets, peeled and very finely shredded
> • ½ cup honey
> • Juice from 2 lemons
> • 4 sprigs fresh mint (optional)

Bring the water to a boil in a heavy saucepan. Add the beets, honey, and lemon juice, and return to a boil. Remove the pan from the heat and allow the mixture to steep for 20 minutes. Strain and serve over ice with a sprig of mint in each glass, if desired.

Lentil Nut Patties
with Mushroom Vinaigrette

A CRIMINI MUSHROOM vinaigrette lends moisture and sophistication to these flavorful lentil nut patties. It is interesting to see how the ginger flavor blooms if the patty mixture is left to sit overnight before cooking.

- *2 tablespoons olive oil*
- *¼ large yellow onion, peeled and minced*
- *1 clove garlic, peeled and minced*
- *1 small carrot, peeled and diced*
- *Pinch of dried thyme*
- *Pinch of powdered ginger*
- *1½ cups Spiced Lentils (see page 57), at room temperature*
- *1 cup finely chopped walnuts*
- *¼ cup Vegetable Stock (see page 180) or water, if necessary to thin the batter*
- *Salt to taste*
- *Freshly ground black pepper to taste*
- *Mushroom Vinaigrette (recipe follows)*

Heat 1 tablespoon of the olive oil in a skillet over medium-high heat. Add the onion, garlic, and carrot, and sauté for 5 minutes, stirring constantly. Add the thyme and ginger and sauté gently for 2 minutes, until the vegetables are softened but not browned. Remove the pan from the heat and allow to cool.

Place 1 cup of the cooked lentils in the work bowl of a food processor and purée into a paste. Remove the lentils from the processor and place in a large mixing bowl. Add the walnuts, mixing well, then add the remaining lentils. If the mixture appears too dry or thick, add the vegetable stock, 1 tablespoon at a time, until the lentil batter is easy to handle yet not too moist or thin. Season with salt and pepper.

Divide the mixture into 8 equal portions and form into round patties. Heat the remaining oil in the skillet over medium-high heat and sauté the patties for 2 minutes on each side. Remove the patties from the pan, drain on kitchen towels, and keep warm. Serve with Mushroom Vinaigrette.

• *4 appetizer or 2 main course servings*

mushroom vinaigrette

I CHOSE CRIMINIS for this recipe because they have better flavor than the paler button mushrooms and are becoming more commonly available in supermarkets. For even more vibrant flavor, try chanterelles or morels.

• *¼ cup olive oil*
• *2 cups crimini mush-rooms, washed, dried, and thinly sliced*
• *¼ large yellow onion, peeled and finely diced*
• *1 clove garlic, peeled and minced*
• *2 tablespoons champagne vinegar (malt vinegar or* *apple cider vinegar may be substituted)*
• *1 tablespoon minced fresh basil leaves*
• *1 tablespoon minced fresh parsley leaves*
• *Salt to taste*
• *Freshly ground black pepper to taste*

Heat the olive oil in a large skillet over medium-high heat. Add the mushrooms, onion, and garlic, and sauté until soft, stirring constantly, about 7 minutes. Remove the pan from the heat, place the mushroom mixture in the bowl of a food processor, and blend on high speed until creamy, about 1 minute. Add the vinegar, basil, and parsley, and blend for 15 seconds. Season with salt and pepper and serve warm or cold as an accompaniment to the Lentil Nut Patties.

Makes 2 cups

PEAS

Civilization has benefited from the high protein content of dried peas since ancient times, but it was only in the sixteenth century that tender pea varieties that could be eaten fresh were developed. Today, most of the fresh peas sold in our markets are the green (or English) variety: round, sweet peas enclosed in bulging, inedible pods. Also available are snow peas (known in some places as sugar peas or Chinese pea pods) and sugar snaps, both of which are eaten whole—pod and all—and are sometimes referred to by their French name mange tout, which translates to "eat it all." Sometimes available in American cities with large Chinese populations are fresh pea shoots, which are the tender leaves of young pea plants that were not allowed to flower or produce fruit. If you spot these delicious greens in a market, incorporate them into a salad.

Whereas fresh peas boast a delicate, sweet flavor, dried peas are nutty and robust. Most dried peas in the United States are sold skinned and split, an unfortunate reality since whole dried peas—the main ingredient in the "pease porridge" of nursery rhyme fame—are higher in fiber and more flavorful. Split peas do not need to be soaked, but whole peas should be soaked overnight.

- 1 tablespoon olive oil
- 1 large yellow onion, finely diced
- 1 medium bay leaf
- 3 cups shelled fresh peas
- 3 cups Chicken Stock (see page 181)
- 2 cups plain yogurt
- ¼ cup shredded fresh mint leaves

Heat the oil in a large, heavy saucepan over medium-high heat. Add the onion and bay leaf and sauté until the onion is translucent, about 3 minutes. Add the peas and stock to the pan and bring to a boil. Reduce the heat, cover, and simmer for 3 minutes. Remove the pan from the heat and discard the bay leaf.

Place the stock mixture and yogurt in a food processor and purée for about 2 minutes. Strain into a serving bowl (this soup should be smooth) and chill for at least 2 hours. Sprinkle mint on each portion before serving.

4 appetizer servings

Braised Peas with Lettuce and Pearl Onions

To give this traditional French dish a completely different flavor, try adding 1 bulb of crushed lemon grass, ½ teaspoon ground star anise or anise seeds, or 1 tablespoon shredded mint to the basic stock during the last minute of cooking. Serve as an accompaniment to meat or fish.

- 1 cup Chicken Stock (see page 181) or Vegetable Stock (see page 180)
- 1 cup pearl onions, peeled
- 1 tablespoon sugar
- Pinch of salt
- 2 cups shelled fresh peas
- 1 head Bibb lettuce, washed and finely shredded
- 1 teaspoon extra-virgin olive oil
- 1 teaspoon flour

Place the stock in a large sauté pan and bring to a boil. Add the onions, sugar, and salt, cover, and cook over medium heat for 4 minutes. Add the peas, return to a boil, and cook until the liquid coats the peas and looks glassy, about 2 minutes total. Remove the pan from the heat and add the shredded lettuce.

Mix the olive oil and flour together in a small ramekin to form a smooth paste.

Return the pan to medium heat, slowly stir in the flour paste, and continue to stir until the liquid thickens slightly. Remove the pan from the heat and serve immediately.

4 to 6 side dish servings

Cucumber and Yellow Split Pea Soup

- ¼ cup canola oil
- 1 large yellow onion, peeled and finely diced
- 1 medium baking potato, peeled and finely diced
- 1 cup dried yellow split peas
- Pinch of turmeric
- 1 teaspoon cumin
- 1 teaspoon salt
- ½ teaspoon freshly ground black pepper
- 4 cups Chicken Stock (see page 181)
- 2 cups peeled, seeded, and finely diced English or Burpless cucumber (standard domestic cucumber may be substituted)
- Juice of 1 lime
- 2 tablespoons minced fresh cilantro leaves

Heat the oil in a heavy pot over medium-high heat. Add the onion and potato and sauté for 5 minutes, stirring continuously. Add the peas, turmeric, cumin, salt, pepper, and stock and bring to a boil. Reduce the heat, cover, and simmer for 30 minutes, stirring occasionally. Add the cucumber and continue cooking for 10 minutes. Remove the soup from the heat.

Add the lime juice and cilantro to the soup. Purée the soup in a food processor if a smooth consistency is preferred. This is not meant to be a thin soup, but if it is overly thick, dilute it with chicken stock. Serve either hot or cold.

6 appetizer servings

CHICK-PEAS

The ancient Romans thought chick-peas looked like rams' heads with curling horns, but in modern times they are more simply likened to small hazelnuts. They have a nutty, faintly chestnutlike flavor and a texture so firm that they are nearly impossible to overcook. In the United States, buff-colored chick-peas are the norm, but in India there are red, black, and brown varieties.

Chick-peas have been around since about 5,000 B.C. and are used today in many countries—from Spain through Turkey and the Middle East into India. They are the key ingredient in Middle Eastern hummus (the dip made with chick-peas and sesame paste) and falafel (fried chick-pea patties), and in India are eaten fresh in salads and stir-fries, and as a snack (fresh chick-peas are unavailable in the United States); when dried, they are combined with potatoes, tomatoes, and yogurt and other sauces, or are roasted and ground into a flour that is employed in batters for vegetable fritters and other savory foods.

Some recipes call for removing the skin of the chick-peas after they are cooked, but this is not really crucial. Chick-peas are also referred to as garbanzos (their Spanish name) and ceci (their Italian name).

Chick-Peas

As CHICK-PEAS render a lot of starchy residue, they need to be drained and rinsed after they are boiled for the first time (before they are combined with other ingredients). Use these chick-peas as the basis for other recipes, or try tossing them with pasta or in salads for added texture and nutrition.

> - *1 cup dried chick-peas*
> - *½ large yellow onion, peeled and chopped*
> - *1 clove garlic, peeled and minced*
> - *1 medium bay leaf*
> - *Pinch of salt*
> - *Pinch of freshly ground black pepper*

Place the chick-peas in a colander and pick over to remove any stones or discolored beans. Put the beans in a large stockpot, cover with fresh cold water, and soak for at least 3 hours or preferably overnight to expedite the cooking process.

Drain the beans and cover with fresh water. Bring to a boil, then remove from the heat, drain, and rinse under cold running water. Return the beans to the pot and cover with fresh water again. Add the onion, garlic, bay leaf, salt, and pepper, and bring to a simmer over medium-low heat. Simmer, covered, for 1 hour or until the beans are tender, skimming the surface of the stock from time to time to remove any scum that may have formed. Drain the beans, then return to the pot. Cover and keep warm until ready to serve.

Makes 2 cups

Chick-Pea and Baby Beet Salad with Mustard Seeds and Green Peppercorns

IN MOST CASES baby beets have a sweeter and more intense flavor than "adult" beets. For another wonderful salad, toss cooked and peeled baby beets with a small, finely chopped Vidalia onion, 2 cloves minced garlic, a bit of malt vinegar, a drizzling of olive oil, and crushed black pepper.

- *12 baby beets (1 to 1½ inches in diameter)*
- *1 teaspoon turmeric*
- *1 teaspoon salt*
- *2 tablespoons canola oil*
- *1 tablespoon black mustard seeds*
- *1 teaspoon green peppercorns*
- *1 cup cooked, drained Chick-Peas (see page 65)*
- *1 tablespoon sugar*

Remove the stems from the beets, then wash the beets under running water to remove any dirt. Place the beets in a large, heavy saucepan with the turmeric and salt and cover with water. Bring to a boil and cook, uncovered, for about 12 minutes or until the beets are tender and can be easily pierced with a fork. Remove the beets from the heat and drain. Place the beets in a clean bowl and cover with cold water. Let the beets rest in the cold water for 5 minutes, then peel with your fingers, place on a clean plate, and set aside.

Heat the oil in a large, heavy pan over medium-high heat. Add the mustard seeds and cook until they stop sputtering, about 15 seconds. Add the peppercorns and cook for 30 seconds, then add the peeled beets followed by the chick-peas. Stir in the sugar. Cook until the beets are glazed, about 1 minute. Remove from the pan and serve immediately as a warm salad, or chill and serve as a cold salad.

4 to 6 salad servings

Hummus with Roasted Garlic and Warm Herb Crêpes

HERE I ADD roasted garlic, mellower than raw garlic, to the traditional Middle Eastern hummus recipe. Also, instead of using pita bread to scoop up the hummus, I use herb-speckled crêpes, which are lighter and more flavorful.

- 2 cups cooked Chick-Peas (see page 65)
- ⅓ cup tahini (sesame seed paste)
- ⅓ cup olive oil
- 4 cloves peeled Roasted Garlic (see page 181)
- 2 cloves raw garlic, peeled and minced
- Juice of 1 large lemon
- Pinch of cayenne pepper
- Pinch of cumin
- Pinch of coriander
- Freshly ground black pepper to taste
- Salt to taste
- 1 tablespoon chopped fresh parsley
- Herb Crêpes (recipe follows)

Place the chick-peas in a fine sieve and rinse under cold running water. Drain.

In a food processor, blend the chick-peas and tahini into a fine paste. Add the remaining ingredients except the parsley and blend on high for 1 minute. If the mixture is too thick, dilute with a little water or additional lemon juice to taste. Transfer the hummus to a serving bowl and sprinkle parsley on top before serving with the Herb Crêpes.

Makes 4 appetizer servings

herb crêpes

- ¼ cup rolled oats
- 2 tablespoons millet seeds (optional)
- ⅓ cup rye flour
- 2 tablespoons all-purpose flour
- 2 whole eggs, beaten together
- 2 cups whole milk
- Pinch of herbes de Provence (mix of dried herbs available in specialty food shops)
- ¼ cup butter

Combine the oats, millet seeds (if using), and rye and all-purpose flours in a mixing bowl. Fold in the eggs and gradually add the milk until you have a smooth batter. Mix in the herbs. Allow the batter to stand for 1 hour before using.

Melt 1 tablespoon of the butter in a small nonstick skillet over medium heat. Ladle a ¼-cup portion of batter into the pan and cook until the underside is a light golden brown. Turn and cook the other side. Cover cooked crêpes and keep warm until serving. Continue making crêpes until all of the batter has been used. Serve immediately with Hummus with Roasted Garlic.

Dilled Salmon with Chick-Peas and Scallions

THE SALMON FOR THIS RECIPE is lightly cured in order to give it a firmer texture. It is then seared and served with the chick-peas and scallions.

dilled salmon

- ½ cup sugar
- ½ cup salt
- 1 cup chopped fresh dill
- 1 pound boned and skinned fillet of fresh salmon

chick-peas and scallions

- 1 cup dried chick-peas
- 2 tablespoons virgin olive oil
- 6 large scallions, whites and greens, minced
- 1 clove garlic, peeled and minced
- 4 tablespoons fresh lemon juice
- Pinch of freshly ground black pepper
- Pinch of salt

Combine the sugar, salt, and dill in a flat dish or tray. Place the salmon in the dish and cover with the dill mixture, rubbing the mixture into the fish with your hands. Place a saucepan of equal size and filled with water on top of the fish and leave for 2 hours. Remove the saucepan and wash the fish under cold running water for 10 minutes. Pat the salmon dry on kitchen towels and refrigerate until ready to cook.

Place the chick-peas in a colander and pick over to remove any stones or discolored peas. Put the chick-peas in a large stockpot, cover with fresh cold water, and soak for at least 3 hours or preferably overnight to expedite the cooking process.

Drain the chick-peas and cover with fresh water. Bring to a boil, then remove from the heat, drain, and rinse under cold running water. Return the chick-peas to the pot, cover with fresh water, and simmer over medium-low heat, covered, for 1 hour or until the beans are tender, skimming the surface from time to time to remove any scum that may have formed. Drain the chick-peas, then return to the pot. Cover and keep warm.

Remove the salmon from the refrigerator. Slice the salmon across the fillet into 4 equal pieces. Heat the olive oil in a heavy skillet over high heat. Add the fish fillets and sear for approximately 30 seconds on each side. Remove the fish from the pan and keep warm. Add the scallions and garlic to the pan and sauté for 1 minute. Add the chick-peas, lemon juice, pepper, and salt, and stir to mix thoroughly. Divide the salmon fillets among 4 plates, top with the Chick-Peas and Scallions, and serve immediately.

4 main course servings

Socca

THIS CHICK-PEA crêpe is a specialty of Nice in the south of France, where it is baked in large, flat, round pans and sold by street vendors. I like to serve *socca* in wedges or stuff it with such fillings as ratatouille, fresh sautéed vegetables, cheese, or herbs.

- 1½ *cups chick-pea flour*
- ⅔ *cup virgin olive oil*
- ½ *teaspoon salt*
- *Pinch of herbes de Provence (mixture of*   *dried herbs available in specialty food stores)*
- *Freshly ground black pepper to taste*

Combine the chick-pea flour, ⅓ cup of the oil, salt, herbes de Provence, and 2 cups water in a bowl and mix to a rough batter. Allow the mixture to rest for about 1 hour.

Preheat the broiler.

Ladle ¼ cup of the batter into a flat, round, 8-inch, nonstick ovenproof pan so that it forms a layer ⅛ inch thick on the bottom of the pan. Place the pan under the broiler for about 3 minutes. Remove the pan from the heat, sprinkle with 1 teaspoon olive oil, then return to the oven for 5 minutes or until the *socca* is a crisp golden brown. Sprinkle the *socca* with pepper to taste, slide onto a plate, and keep warm until serving. Repeat until all of the batter has been used (about 8 *soccas* in all). Cut each *socca* into wedges and serve.

4 appetizer or side dish servings

BLACK-EYED PEAS

I've never come across a food with so many aliases. What I call black-eyed peas are known to others as black-eyed beans, black-eyed Suzies, Southern peas, lady peas, cream peas, brown-eyed peas, crowder peas, cow peas, China beans, and marble beans. Fortunately, most other facts about these slightly elongated legumes marked with a single black dot are less controversial.

They are believed to have originated in China, from where they traveled to the Middle East and Africa. Introduced into the United States by African slaves, they achieved their greatest acceptance in the South, where they are still a staple. Appreciated for their buttery texture and mild, pealike flavor, they are combined with rice to make the famous Southern New Year's Day specialty called Hoppin' John, as well as similar Southeast Asian and Senegalese dishes. In Martinique they are featured in a spicy fritter called acras de zieu noi's, *traditionally eaten on Good Friday. They are also a key ingredient—both whole and split and husked—in many dishes of southwestern India.*

Black-Eyed Peas Thermidor

THE LOWLY BLACK-EYED PEA, so popular among Southern-ers, takes the place of lobster in this surprising takeoff on a classic French preparation.

Place the black-eyed peas in a colander and pick over to remove any stones or discol-ored peas. Put the peas in a small stockpot, cover with fresh cold water, and soak for at least 3 hours or prefer-ably overnight to expedite the cooking process.

Drain the peas, return them to the pot, and cover with the chicken stock. Using the clove as a pin, attach the bay leaf to the whole onion. Add the studded onion to the pot and bring to a boil. Reduce the heat and cook, uncovered, until the peas are tender, about 45 minutes to 1 hour. Drain the peas, reserving the stock in a clean bowl. Discard the studded onion. Return the peas to the pot and cover.

Place the mustard powder in a small bowl and gradually mix in 1 teaspoon of water or cream to make a loose paste (add more water if needed). Fold the mustard paste, ½ cup of the Parmesan cheese, and the cooked spinach into the reserved chicken stock. Mix the chicken stock mix-ture back into the peas, then fold in the cream. Mix well. Season with salt and pepper.

Preheat the oven to 400° F.

Pour the peas into a casse-role dish. Sprinkle the top of the peas with the remaining Parmesan cheese and bake for 30 minutes or until the cheese browns. Remove from the oven and serve immediately.

4 appetizer or side dish servings

- 1 cup dried black-eyed peas
- 3 cups Chicken Stock (see page 181)
- 1 clove
- 1 medium bay leaf
- 1 medium yellow onion, peeled
- 2 tablespoons dry English mustard powder
- ½ cup heavy cream
- 1 cup grated Parmesan cheese
- ½ cup cooked and drained spinach leaves or collard greens
- Salt to taste
- Freshly ground black pepper to taste

Grains

CORN AND CORN PRODUCTS

According to food historians, wild corn may have been growing in southern Mexico as early as 5200 B.C., cultivated corn in 3400 B.C. Corn was so sacred to the Mayans that they used human blood to fertilize it. Columbus was introduced to corn by the Arawaks in the Caribbean, and when settlers arrived in the New World the Native Americans taught them how to cultivate and cook corn as well as grind it to make cornmeal. Back in Europe, corn never became popular for more than animal feed except in isolated pockets, such as Northern Italy, where polenta (cooked cornmeal) is a dietary staple.

Interestingly, in English-speaking countries outside of North America, "maize" is the word for corn, and "corn" is the word used for whatever is the most popular grain, such as wheat in England and oats in Ireland and Scotland.

Sweet corn, of which there are many varieties, is the type of corn served on the cob and preserved by canning and freezing. It is picked when immature while the kernels are still sweet and juicy. Field corn (also known as dent corn) is picked when mature and starchy, then dried. (Ninety percent of the field corn in this country is used as livestock feed; the remainder is used in processed foods and drinks as well as non-food products, such as plastic and fuel.) Popcorn is a field-type corn with a very hard hull; when heated, the kernel's internal moisture becomes steam and because the steam has nowhere to go it causes the kernel to explode. Indian (or flint) corn, with its multicolored kernels, is the type used as decoration in the fall; blue corn, which was nearly extinct in the United States in the beginning of the 1980s, is now a featured ingredient in tortillas, cornbread, and pancake mixes, and is also sold as cornmeal.

Corn on the Cob

WHEN I FIRST TASTED corn on the cob as a boy in England I was surprised by the sweetness of the kernels, especially when slathered with butter. It was so strangely American in concept, and I remember imagining as I ate it what it would be like to live on a farm in Kansas.

Today I add milk to the liquid in which I cook corn in order to keep the kernels from becoming bitter. For variation, I like to serve corn with different toppings, such as flavored olive oils, soy sauce, or maple syrup, and / or cook it in the husk on the grill until the husk is slightly brown.

- *1 gallon water*
- *1 quart milk*
- *4 tablespoons (½ stick) unsalted butter*
- *2 tablespoons sugar*
- *1 teaspoon salt*
- *1 teaspoon red pepper flakes (optional)*
- *12 ears fresh corn, shucked and silk removed*
- *Butter, olive oil, soy sauce, or maple syrup, for serving (optional)*

Place the water, milk, butter, sugar, salt, and red pepper flakes in a large, heavy pot and bring to a rolling boil over high heat. Add the corn, reduce the heat to a simmer, cover, and cook until tender, about 5 to 8 minutes. Remove the pot from the heat and let stand until needed.

Drain and serve hot, either plain or with the condiments of your choosing, such as oil, butter, or maple syrup.

12 side dish servings

Corn and Six-Pepper Relish

THIS RELISH is especially good when matched with grilled fish or poultry. I enjoy the contrast between the sweet green peppercorns (the soft underripe berries of the pepper plant) and the sharp, hot Szechwan peppercorns (the dried berries of the prickly ash tree). To make this relish spicy, do not seed one or more of the jalapeños.

- *4 cups fresh corn kernels (approximately 6 ears of corn)*
- *1½ cups champagne vinegar (malt or apple cider vinegar may be used)*
- *2½ cups sugar*
- *1 teaspoon freshly ground black pepper*
- *1 teaspoon freshly ground green peppercorns*
- *1 teaspoon dried mustard powder*
- *1 teaspoon ground turmeric*
- *½ red onion, peeled and finely diced*
- *1 large yellow bell pepper, seeded and diced*
- *1 large red bell pepper, seeded and diced*
- *1 large green bell pepper, seeded and diced*
- *1 tablespoon freshly ground Szechwan peppercorns*
- *3 fresh jalapeño peppers, seeded and finely diced*

In a large saucepan over medium-high heat, bring the corn, vinegar, sugar, black pepper, green peppercorns, mustard powder, turmeric, and onion to a boil. Simmer for 10 minutes.

Add the bell peppers, Szechwan peppercorns, and jalapeño peppers to the pot and simmer for 20 minutes. Remove the pot from the heat and cool to room temperature. Transfer the relish into an airtight container and refrigerate until ready to use. It will keep for up to 3 days.

Makes 2 cups

Corn, Crab, and Basil Soup
with Corn Fritters

CORN IS AMONG my all-time favorite vegetables, so when it is in season I like to incorporate it into all sorts of dishes. Here, I combine it with crabmeat to create a delicious basil- and wine-scented soup that is simultaneously chunky (thanks to the corn) and smooth (thanks to the finely chopped potato, which falls apart as it cooks). To accompany the corn, I devised a simple recipe for corn fritters lightly seasoned with marjoram, an herb that belongs to the mint family but actually boasts a mild, oregano-like flavor.

Heat the oil over medium-high heat in a large, heavy stock-pot. Add the onion, potato, garlic, and bay leaf, and sauté for 5 minutes or until the onion becomes transparent. Add the corn, basil, chicken stock, and white wine, and bring to a rolling boil. Cook for 10 minutes, stirring from time to time. Add the crabmeat, heavy cream, salt, and white pepper, and continue cooking over high heat for an additional 10 minutes, stirring to prevent the soup from sticking to the pan.

Remove the pan from the heat, adjust the seasoning to taste, and serve hot with Corn Fritters.

6 appetizer or 4 main course servings

- ¼ *cup virgin olive oil*
- *1 large yellow onion, peeled and finely chopped*
- *1 large potato, peeled and finely chopped*
- *1 large clove garlic, peeled and minced*
- *1 medium bay leaf*
- *4 cups fresh corn kernels (approximately 6 ears of corn)*
- ¼ *cup shredded fresh basil leaves*
- *4 cups Chicken Stock (see page 181)*
- ½ *cup dry white wine or vermouth*
- *1 pound lump crabmeat*
- *1 cup heavy cream*
- ¼ *teaspoon salt*
- ¼ *teaspoon white pepper*
- *Corn Fritters (recipe follows)*

corn fritters

IF YOU DON'T have a potato masher, use a strong fork to mash the corn kernels.

Use a potato masher to crush the corn kernels. In a mixing bowl, combine the crushed corn, egg yolks, flour, marjoram, and salt. Stir well to blend.

Pour ¼ inch of oil into a small, heavy skillet and place over medium-high heat. Form the fritters by dropping the batter in 1-tablespoon portions into the pan, then fry the fritters until golden brown, about 2 minutes on each side. Cook the fritters in batches, adding more oil to the pan as necessary. Drain on paper towels and serve immediately with Corn, Crab, and Basil Soup.

- *1 cup fresh corn kernels (about 2 ears of corn)*
- *3 large egg yolks, well beaten*
- ½ *cup all-purpose flour*
- *1 teaspoon dried marjoram*
- ¼ *teaspoon salt*
- *Vegetable oil, for frying*

Makes 8 to 12 fritters

Cornmeal-Battered Portobello Mushrooms with Spiced Cashew Sauce or Cilantro-Tamari Dipping Sauce

WHEN PREPARED WITH LARGE MUSHROOMS, this dish makes an excellent vegetarian main course (serve two mushrooms per person). For appetizer portions, cut the mushrooms into halves or quarters after cooking. If neither the Cashew Sauce nor the Cilantro-Tamari Dipping Sauce appeals to you, try dusting the mushrooms with freshly ground black pepper before serving.

Trim the mushrooms and remove the stems. Peel the top layer of skin from the mushrooms and discard. Lightly season the mushrooms with salt and black pepper.

To make the batter, place the cornmeal, ¼ cup of the flour, the half-and-half, eggs, five-spice powder, red pepper flakes, salt, and black pepper in a large bowl and combine with a hand mixer.

- 8 medium portobello mushrooms
- 1¼ cups cornmeal
- ½ cup all-purpose flour
- 2 cups half-and-half
- 2 whole eggs
- Pinch of five-spice powder
- 1 teaspoon red pepper flakes
- ½ teaspoon salt, plus extra for seasoning the mushrooms
- ¼ teaspoon black pepper, plus extra for seasoning the mushrooms
- ¼ cup canola or vegetable oil
- Spiced Cashew Sauce or Cilantro-Tamari Dipping Sauce (recipes follow)

Preheat the oven to 350° F.

Set a heavy skillet over medium-high heat and coat with a film of oil. Dust the mushrooms with the remaining ¼ cup flour and dip into the batter. Place the batter-dipped mushrooms in the hot skillet one at a time and brown on both sides, about 2 minutes per side. Remove the browned mushrooms to an ungreased baking sheet and cook in the oven for 10 to 12 minutes, until they spring back when pressed with a finger.

Drain the mushrooms on clean towels and, if desired, cut each one into halves or quarters. Place on serving plates and serve immediately with Spiced Cashew Sauce or Cilantro-Tamari Dipping Sauce.

8 appetizer or 4 main course servings

spiced cashew sauce

Place the cashews on a roasting sheet in a 300° F oven and warm through, about 5 minutes.

Measure 1 tablespoon of the canola oil into a small pan set over medium heat. Add the garlic and sauté until soft but not browned, about 1 minute. Remove from the heat.

Place all of the ingredients, including the warm nuts and garlic, in a food processor and blend on high speed for

- *1 cup unsalted roasted cashews (see Note)*
- *3 tablespoons canola or vegetable oil*
- *2 large cloves garlic, peeled and minced*
- *2 tablespoons peeled and finely chopped fresh gingerroot*
- *2 tablespoons honey*
- *2 tablespoons rice wine vinegar*
- *1 tablespoon sesame oil*
- *2 teaspoons chili oil*
- *2 tablespoons finely chopped fresh cilantro leaves*
- *1 teaspoon sugar*

45 seconds. If the mixture is too thick, dilute with water to desired consistency. Serve with the Cornmeal-Battered Portobello Mushrooms.

Note: If unsalted cashews are unavailable, use salted ones. To remove the salt, sauté the nuts for 10 seconds in 2 tablespoons vegetable oil, then remove the nuts from the pan with a slotted spoon and drain on paper towels.

Makes 2 cups

cilantro-tamari dipping sauce

- *¼ cup champagne vinegar (malt or cider vinegar may be substituted)*
- *2 tablespoons tamari*
- *½ clove garlic, peeled and finely chopped*
- *½ teaspoon crushed red pepper flakes*
- *1 teaspoon finely chopped fresh cilantro leaves*

Combine all of the ingredients and serve as a dip for the Cornmeal-Battered Portobello Mushrooms.

Makes ⅓ cup

Grit Cakes
with Poached Eggs

I GOT THE IDEA for this recipe when I was the chef at the Windsor Court Hotel in New Orleans. At the end of the breakfast service we would almost always be faced with a pot of leftover grits. Rather than throwing them away, I decided to try to make cakes out of them. My experiment proved successful, and I now use these grit cakes as a savory base for poached eggs as well as maple syrup and fresh fruit, such as peaches, strawberries, or apricots. I also serve them as an accompaniment to lamb and other meat dishes (in place of mashed potatoes or polenta).

- 1 cup coarse grits
- 1 tablespoon unsalted butter
- 2 egg yolks
- 3 tablespoons canola oil
- ½ cup grated Cheddar cheese
- 1 jalapeño pepper, finely diced
- 1 tablespoon finely diced green bell pepper
- Pinch of salt
- ½ teaspoon freshly ground black pepper
- 8 Poached Eggs (recipe follows)

Bring 5 cups water to a rolling boil in a large, heavy saucepan over high heat. Slowly add the grits, stirring constantly. Reduce the heat to low, cover the pan, and simmer the grits for 30 minutes, stirring occasionally to prevent lumps from forming. Remove the pan from the heat and quickly fold in the butter and egg yolks, stirring with a wooden spoon. Grease a 6-by-9-inch baking pan with 1 tablespoon of the oil. Add the cheese, diced jalapeño and bell peppers, salt, and pepper to the grits and mix well. Pour the mixture into the greased pan and allow to cool.

Cut the grits into 8 squares and remove from the pan.

Heat the remaining 2 tablespoons oil in a heavy nonstick skillet over medium-high heat. Add the grit squares in batches and sauté until golden brown, about 1 minute on each side.

Remove the cakes from the skillet and drain on kitchen towels. Serve immediately with a poached egg on top of each cake, 2 cakes and eggs per person.

4 main course servings

poached eggs

CREATING A "whirlpool" in the water before adding the eggs facilitates the whites wrapping around the yolks as the eggs cook, which is particularly helpful if the eggs are not at their peak of freshness. Adding vinegar and salt to the water helps the whites coagulate; however, the salt can be omitted if desired.

- 2 tablespoons white wine vinegar
- Pinch of salt
- 8 eggs

Bring 1 quart water to a simmer in a large, heavy saucepan over medium-high heat. Add the vinegar and salt to the water. Remove the pan from the heat and, with a spoon, stir to form a whirlpool in the water. Carefully crack the eggs one by one into the center of the whirlpool (restarting the whirlpool if necessary), return the pan to the heat, and poach the eggs for 3 minutes. Remove the eggs with a slotted spoon and drain on kitchen towels. Serve immediately on top of the Grit Cakes.

Polenta Pizza

crust

IN THIS PIZZA RECIPE, I substitute polenta for the usual flour-dough crust. If desired, enrich the crust with fresh, full-flavored herbs, such as rosemary, oregano, basil, or thyme. Or, instead of making pizza, pour the cooked polenta into a pie pan and chill. When it is firm, cut the polenta into wedges, quickly sauté in a little oil, and serve as an alternative to bread, potatoes, or rice.

- 2 cups milk
- 1 cup water
- 1 medium bay leaf
- ½ teaspoon salt
- ¼ teaspoon white pepper
- 1 cup yellow cornmeal
- ½ cup grated Parmesan cheese
- 4 tablespoons butter
- ½ cup virgin olive oil (reserve any leftover oil to use as a topping)

In a heavy saucepan, bring the milk, water, bay leaf, salt, and white pepper to a low boil. When the mixture reaches a boil, add the cornmeal, stirring vigorously with a wooden spoon to avoid lumps. When all of the cornmeal is incorporated, reduce the heat to low and continue stirring for 25 to 30 minutes, until the polenta pulls away from the sides of the pan or a finger pressed gently into the polenta comes out clean.

When the mixture is smooth, remove the pan from the heat and add the cheese and butter. Pour the batter into a flat pan and allow to cool. Divide into 4 equal portions of about 1 cup each, placing each portion between 2 sheets of plastic wrap. With the heel of your hand or with a rolling pin, press each portion of polenta into a circle about 6 to 7 inches in diameter. Remove the circles from the plastic wrap and set aside.

Preheat the oven to 350° F.

Heat a large, heavy skillet over medium-high heat and coat with 2 tablespoons of the oil. Slide one of the polenta crusts into the skillet and cook gently until the underside turns light golden brown. Turn carefully and repeat, cooking about 4 minutes on the second side. Repeat with each crust and place on a large baking sheet. If desired, refrigerate or freeze crusts for later use.

toppings

In a large bowl, combine the 4 cheeses. Divide the tomato slices among the pizza crusts, then sprinkle the cheeses on top. Place the pizzas in the preheated oven and cook for 10 to 12 minutes or until the cheese begins to

- ½ cup crumbled goat cheese
- ½ cup grated Parmesan cheese
- ½ cup grated provolone cheese
- ½ cup grated mozzarella cheese
- 6 large Italian plum tomatoes, sliced crosswise into rounds
- 20 black olives, pits removed
- 4 tablespoons shredded fresh basil leaves
- 10 anchovy fillets (optional)

bubble. Remove the pizzas from the oven and garnish with the olives, basil, and anchovies, (if using). Drizzle each pizza lightly with the remaining olive oil and serve immediately.

4 main course servings

Sweet Vanilla Polenta

HERE I HAVE ADAPTED the savory polenta for a satisfying winter dessert. I chose a finely ground cornmeal for this recipe because I wanted the polenta to be as creamy and smooth as possible.

When cooking polenta make sure that the pan has a very thick bottom and that you stir the cornmeal mixture constantly with a wooden spoon.

- *4 cups skim milk*
- *Pinch of salt*
- *1 vanilla bean, split lengthwise, or 1 teaspoon pure vanilla extract*
- *1 cup finely ground cornmeal*
- *½ cup sugar*
- *½ cup Mascarpone cheese or strawberry or apricot preserves (optional)*

Combine the milk, salt, and vanilla bean halves (if using) in a large, heavy saucepan. Bring the mixture to a boil over high heat, then reduce to a simmer. Slowly add the corn-meal, stirring constantly, and cook, continuing to stir, for 5 to 7 minutes. Remove the pan from the heat, stir in the sugar and vanilla extract (if using), and allow the polenta to sit, covered, for 5 minutes. Remove the vanilla bean halves, if necessary.

Divide the polenta among 6 to 8 dessert dishes. If desired, spoon a large dollop of Mas-carpone cheese or straw-berry or apricot preserves in the center of each serving.

6 to 8 dessert servings

MILLET

The oldest of grains, millet has been around since the Neolithic age—at least. It is referred to in the Old Testament as "the gruel of endurance," was grown in the hanging gardens of Babylon, and today is widely consumed in Asia and Africa. In the United States, however, this hearty grain, which can survive even in dry and underfertilized soil, has always nourished more birds and livestock than human beings. The millet used for cooking, unlike the animal food, is hulled and stripped of its outer bran layer, which is indigestible.

Available in health-food and Asian grocery stores, millet grains are tiny, spherical, pale yellow to reddish orange in color, and have a delicate, mildly nutlike flavor. They can be cooked in liquid, without stirring, until the grains are fluffy and separate with a fine texture similar to couscous. Or, they can be cooked by adding liquid gradually and stirring until porridgelike. Their delicate flavor combines readily with fresh fruit and vegetables.

Nutritionally powerful, millet equals or surpasses wheat in protein content (depending on the variety) and is higher in B vitamins, copper, and iron than whole wheat and brown rice. Millet can also usually be tolerated by people who are allergic to wheat.

Finely ground millet is used by Ethiopians to make a fermented, spongy, flat bread called injera (another grain, called teff, is also used), by Indians to make crepe-like roti, and by a Masai tribe in Africa to make beer for consumption and for trading. Because millet produces no gluten (the protein that gives dough strength and elasticity), it cannot be used on its own to make raised breads.

Millet Cakes
with Tomato Vinaigrette

MY FIRST EXPOSURE to millet cakes was at a health-food store, where I bought the prepackaged variety. I wasn't very impressed by the blandness or dryness but liked the concept so I decided to try to make my own version with fresh ingredients and a vinaigrette for extra flavor and moisture. I enjoy the nutty taste of the millet and the touch of sweetness lent by the dried fruit. If desired, dried cranberries or blueberries can be substituted for the raisins.

- 1 cup millet
- 2½ cups Chicken Stock (see page 181)
- 1 tablespoon raisins
- 2 tablespoons mixed dried fruit
- 1 tablespoon toasted sliced almonds
- Pinch of fresh chopped rosemary
- 2 tablespoons olive oil
- Tomato Vinaigrette (recipe follows)

Place the millet and chicken stock in a large, heavy saucepan and bring to a boil over high heat. Reduce the heat to a simmer, cover, and cook until nearly all the stock has been absorbed, about 20 to 25 minutes. Remove the pan from the heat and allow to stand, covered, for 10 minutes.

Uncover and stir in the raisins, dried fruit, almonds, and rosemary. Cover again and allow to rest for an additional 5 minutes.

Pour the millet mixture into a large mixing bowl and form into 8 to 10 portions of ½ cup each. Squeeze the millet between your hands to make firm balls, then gently flatten to form cakes.

Heat the olive oil in a large, heavy skillet over medium-high heat. Add the millet cakes and sauté gently until golden brown, about 2 minutes per side. Remove the cakes from the pan and keep warm.

Serve with Tomato Vinaigrette.

4 to 5 appetizer servings

tomato vinaigrette

- 4 large beefsteak tomatoes, cored and cut into quarters
- ¼ large yellow onion, peeled
- ¼ cup extra-virgin olive oil
- ⅛ cup champagne vinegar (malt or cider vinegar may be substituted)
- 2 cloves garlic, peeled and chopped
- 10 sprigs fresh tarragon
- ½ teaspoon black pepper
- ½ teaspoon salt

Place all of the ingredients in a blender or food processor and mix for 1 minute on high speed. Remove and serve with the Millet Cakes.

Makes 2½ cups

BARLEY

Barley can be traced back to the Stone Age; in writings of ancient China from around 2800 B.C. it is listed along with rice, millet, soybeans, and wheat as one of the five most sacred cultivated crops. It was the most important grain on the European continent up until the 1500s and has been used at different times in history not only as a food, but as a medication, measuring standard, and form of currency. To this day in Britain, drinking the water that barley is cooked in is said to cure an upset stomach and to promote a silky, smooth complexion. It was carried by colonists to the New World, but then as now it was appreciated more for its role in beer production than as a nutritious and delicious addition to the diet.

There are several different types of barley available in markets today, by far the most prevalent being pearl (or pearled) barley, which is barley from which the double outer husk and bran layer have been removed. This process, which involves six scourings, removes many of barley's nutrients, though the protein content remains relatively high. Also available are quick-cooking barley, which is pearl barley that has been presteamed, reducing the cooking time considerably but not affecting the nutritional profile; pot (or Scotch) barley, which is scoured only three times so that some of the bran remains; and the most nutrient-dense type of barley, called hulled barley, from which only the inedible outer hull has been removed. As expected, the less the barley is processed, the longer the cooking time required and the more its earthy flavor is maintained (compare 1 hour 40 minutes for ½ cup hulled barley to 55 minutes for the same amount of pearl barley).

Braised Pearl Barley with Basil Pesto

THE FLAVOR AND TEXTURE of pearl barley are reminiscent of pasta, especially rice-shaped orzo, but barley does not have the same high starch content. Also, barley absorbs sauces, such as the pesto presented here; it is not simply coated with them.

Serve this side dish warm with grilled meat or seafood.

Place the barley in a fine sieve and wash under cold running water until the water runs clear, about 5 minutes. Drain.

In a heavy saucepan, combine the barley, onion, bay leaf, chicken stock, salt, and pepper. Bring to a boil, then reduce the heat, cover, and simmer for 30 minutes. Remove from the heat and allow to stand for 5 minutes uncovered. Fold in 2 tablespoons of the Basil Pesto and mix well, fluffing with a fork.

6 to 8 side dish servings

- 1 cup pearl barley
- 1 large yellow onion, finely diced
- 1 medium bay leaf
- 3½ cups Chicken Stock (see page 181)
- ½ teaspoon salt
- ½ teaspoon freshly ground black pepper
- 2 tablespoons Basil Pesto (recipe follows)

basil pesto

THE ASCORBIC ACID in the vitamin C tablet helps the pesto maintain its natural green color; without the vitamin C the pesto begins to turn brown quickly, but the flavor is unaffected.

In a blender, combine the garlic, basil, pine nuts, cheeses, and vitamin C pill (if using). Blend on high for 1 minute, then slowly add the oil in a steady stream so that the mixture binds together. Add salt and pepper to taste.

Use with Braised Pearl Barley and refrigerate remainder in an airtight container for up to 2 weeks or freeze to be used as needed in sauces and marinades.

Makes 3 cups

- 10 cloves garlic, peeled
- 1½ cups lightly packed fresh basil leaves, washed and dried
- ⅔ cup roasted pine nuts
- ½ cup freshly grated Parmesan cheese
- ½ cup freshly grated Romano cheese
- 1 vitamin C pill (optional)
- 1 to 1¼ cups extra-virgin olive oil
- Salt to taste
- Freshly ground black pepper to taste

Lemon or Lime Barley Water

A GREAT BRITISH tradition, lemon barley water was a staple in my house when I was growing up. We drank it in particularly prodigious quantities during the few very warm days of summer. It has a smooth, silky taste and is a wonderful thirst quencher or addition to mixed drinks. It has been a primary drink during Wimbledon Week (every June) for as long as I can remember, the players drinking it often when they take their seats by the umpire. Lemon barley water is sold in bottles in the United States but it tastes much better when homemade.

Place 4½ cups water in a heavy pot with the barley and bring to a boil. Reduce the mixture by 50 percent over high heat. Strain the liquid into a clean glass container. Mix in the lemon or lime juice and honey or sugar, stirring well.

Serve well chilled.

2 servings

- *3 tablespoons pearl barley*
- *4 tablespoons freshly squeezed lemon or lime juice*
- *3 tablespoons honey or sugar, or to taste*

Cock-a-Leekie

THE RECIPE FOR cock-a-leekie originated in Scotland. I suspect that it made its way to Nova Scotia and was later taken to Louisiana, where it became gumbo. Serving prunes in cock-a-leekie was popular until the early 1800s. Since not everyone appreciates prunes, I've made them an optional.

- 1 large chicken, 3 to 4 pounds, cleaned
- 2 quarts Chicken Stock (see page 181)
- 1 teaspoon salt
- 1 teaspoon white pepper
- 2 leeks, whites and greens, carefully washed and sliced into ¼-inch rounds
- 2 carrots, peeled and sliced into ¼-inch rounds
- 2 medium bay leaves
- ¼ cup pearl barley
- ¼ cup long-grain rice
- ½ teaspoon fresh thyme
- ½ cup prunes (optional)

Place the chicken in a large stockpot and cover with the chicken stock, salt, and white pepper. Bring to a boil over high heat, lower the heat to a simmer, and cook, covered, until the bird is tender, about 1½ to 2 hours, skimming the surface periodically to remove any scum that rises.

Remove the pot from the heat and transfer the bird to a plate to cool. Skim the stock again to remove any surface scum, then add the remaining ingredients, except the prunes. Return the pot to the heat and simmer the soup for 30 minutes, skimming the surface occasionally.

When the chicken is cool enough to handle, pull the meat from the bones, discarding the skin and bones. Remove the soup from the heat, add the chicken meat, and return to a boil for 2 minutes.

Remove the bay leaves. Season the soup with salt and pepper to taste, add the prunes (if using), and serve.

6 main course servings

WHEAT AND WHEAT PRODUCTS

Nourishing more of the population than any other grain, wheat is the most important cereal crop in the world. It is also among the oldest: The story of its cultivation and processing is told on murals on Egyptian tombs, in ancient Chinese writings, and on bronze tablets from Assyria. Unlike many other cereal grains, such as millet, oats, and corn, wheat is primarily processed into human rather than animal food. It is also the only cereal grain that produces enough of its own gluten (the protein that gives dough strength and elasticity) to make a raised loaf of bread (most other grains need to be mixed and matched to achieve the necessary gluten content). The most common form of wheat is wheat flour, of which there are many varieties, the healthiest being those that are made with all three parts of the wheat kernel: the endosperm (main portion of the kernel, accounting for about 83 percent of its weight) , the germ (embryo or sprouting section of the kernel), and the bran (the outer coating). Whole-wheat flours are made with all three parts. White flours (such as all-purpose and cake flour) are made with the endosperm only.

Other forms of wheat used in cooking include:

Semolina: the coarsely ground endosperm of durum wheat (the hardest kind of wheat), which is used to make the best-quality pasta as well as couscous (small granules of precooked, then dried semolina).

Cracked wheat: the whole wheat kernel broken into small pieces; available in fine, medium, and coarse granulations.

Bulgur: steam-cooked, then dried wheat kernels broken into small pieces; available in fine, medium, and coarse granulations. Bulgur can be cooked in liquid on the stove or by soaking in boiled water. It has a stronger flavor than cracked wheat.

Whole wheat berries (also called groats): whole wheat kernels that have not been milled, polished, or heat-treated. They are round, brown, and boast a strong nutty flavor. They take over an hour to cook, though the cooking time can be shortened by presoaking.

Farina (also known as cream of wheat): endosperm of the wheat grain milled to a fine granular consistency, then sifted; usually enriched with vitamins and minerals and served as breakfast cereal, though it can be used in other ways, such as to make dumplings or desserts. In Greece it is cooked with eggs to create the custard-like filling for the phyllo-dough pastry called galatoboureko.

Rolled wheat (wheat flakes): whole wheat berries that are heated, then flattened between rollers. The flakes are similar to rolled oats but are thicker and firmer. They can be added to baked goods or used to make hot cereal.

Bulgur, Eggplant, and Tomato Napoleons

To FACILITATE THE ASSEMBLY of the napoleons, put the eggplant and tomato slices back in order after cutting and cooking them. To serve the napoleons after baking, cut very carefully lengthwise so that the vegetables are exposed. An electric knife simplifies this task considerably.

Brings 3 cups water to a boil. Place the bulgur in a large mixing bowl and pour the boiling water over it. Allow the bulgur to soak for 1 hour.

Place the olive oil in a large pan and heat over medium-high heat. Add the thyme and rosemary to the oil and sauté for 30 seconds. Add the presoaked bulgur and vegetable stock, lower the heat, and cook for 5 minutes. Adjust the seasoning with salt and pepper to taste, remove the pan from the heat, and allow to cool.

Cut the eggplants lengthwise into ¼-inch-thick slices and, as quickly as possible, rub both sides of each slice with canola oil. Heat a heavy skillet over high heat and quickly cook each slice for 30 seconds on each side. Repeat with all of the slices. Drain the eggplant on kitchen towels.

Cut the tomatoes across the diameter into ¼-inch-thick slices and quickly sear on both sides in the skillet over high heat. Remove the tomatoes to a plate and allow to cool.

Preheat the oven to 400° F.

- 3 cups coarse bulgur wheat
- 3 tablespoons virgin olive oil
- ½ teaspoon fresh thyme
- ¼ teaspoon fresh rosemary
- ½ cup Vegetable Stock (see page 180)
- Salt to taste
- Freshly ground black pepper to taste
- 2 1-pound eggplants, washed and stems removed
- ½ cup canola oil
- 4 large vine-ripened tomatoes, such as Louisiana Creoles or beefsteaks, cores removed
- 1 tablespoon tahini (sesame seed paste)
- 4 tablespoons garlic, mashed into a paste
- Juice of 1 lemon

In a small bowl, combine the tahini, garlic, and lemon juice, and season with salt and black pepper. Lay the eggplant slices out on a baking sheet in the order in which they were cut from the vegetable. Spread each slice with a thin coating of the tahini mixture, top with a tomato slice, then a heaping tablespoon of bulgur wheat. On two separate pieces of aluminum foil, reform the eggplant shape by assembling the slices one on top of another, then tightly wrap each "eggplant" in the aluminum foil. Bake in the preheated oven for 20 minutes.

Remove the "eggplants" from the oven and allow to rest for 5 minutes. Cover each one with a kitchen towel and gently squeeze into shape. Carefully remove the foil, cut very carefully lengthwise so that the vegetables are exposed, and serve immediately.

4 main course or 8 side dish servings

Couscous with Grilled Vegetables and Spinach Sauce

THE BALSAMIC VINEGAR–SUGAR marinade that flavors the vegetables for this dish also helps the vegetables to take on defined grill marks, as the sugar in the marinade caramelizes quickly when it is exposed to the grill heat.

In a small pan, bring the vinegar to a simmer over medium heat. Add the sugar and cook until the sugar completely dissolves, about 5 minutes or more. Remove from the heat and cool.

Place the sliced vegetables flat in a long tray or baking dish and pour on the sugared vinegar. Mix the vegetables around so that all surfaces are covered. Allow to marinate for 1 hour.

Place the stock in a heavy saucepan and bring to a boil. Remove from the heat, stir in the couscous, and cover. Allow to sit for 5 minutes, until all of the liquid is absorbed. Stir in the remaining ingredients through the black pepper and mix with a fork, fluffing up the grains as you toss lightly. Cover again to keep warm.

- 1 cup balsamic vinegar
- 1 cup light brown sugar
- 1 large tomato, cored and cut crosswise into 4 thick slices
- 1 medium eggplant, trimmed and quartered lengthwise
- 1 medium zucchini, trimmed and quartered lengthwise
- 1 medium yellow squash, trimmed and quartered lengthwise
- 1½ cups Chicken Stock (see page 181) or Vegetable Stock (see page 180)
- 1 cup couscous
- 1 tablespoon lemon juice
- 1 tablespoon shredded fresh mint leaves
- 1 tablespoon shredded cilantro leaves
- 2 tablespoons extra-virgin olive oil
- 1 teaspoon freshly ground black pepper
- Spinach Sauce (recipe follows on page 98)

Bring a grill or griddle up to a high temperature (coals on a grill should be grayish white and a griddle should be just below smoking). Place the vegetables on the grill or griddle in a single layer and cook until well-marked, about 2 minutes. (As they cook, the sugar in the vinegar will begin to emit a caramel aroma.) Turn and cook the second side. Repeat with the remaining marinated vegetables, keeping the cooked ones warm.

Spoon the couscous onto 4 serving plates and surround with the grilled vegetables. Pass the Spinach Sauce in a separate bowl at the table.

4 appetizer or side dish servings

spinach sauce

I SUGGEST BAGGED spinach for this sauce because it is generally cleaner than loose leaves. I still advise, however, that you wash the spinach well before beginning the recipe, even adding a little salt to the water as this will make any bugs jump off. I add Pernod and nutmeg to this sauce to bring out the flavor of the spinach. To make a warm dip for pita bread triangles, fold in some grated Swiss cheese.

- 4 tablespoons olive oil
- 2 shallots, finely diced
- 1-pound bag fresh spinach, rinsed well and dried, stems removed
- 1 tablespoon rice wine vinegar
- Pinch of nutmeg
- 1 tablespoon Pernod
- 1 vitamin C pill, crushed (see Note)
- Salt to taste
- Freshly ground black pepper to taste

Heat the oil over high heat in a large sauté pan. Add the shallots and sauté for 1 minute, then add the spinach leaves to the pan. Cover and allow the spinach to "sweat" for 1 minute.

Remove the pan from the heat and place the contents in a food processor along with the remaining ingredients. Process on high until well combined. Season to taste with salt and pepper, and serve with Couscous with Grilled Vegetables.

Note: The vitamin C tablet will slow down the oxidation process, keeping the sauce a nice green color longer.

Makes 1 cup

Crab and Scallion Couscous Cakes with Cucumber Vinaigrette

COUSCOUS, WHICH CAN BE combined with any number of herbs, vegetables, fish, meat, or even fruit, is usually served with a stew or as a side dish or salad. Here I've taken advantage of its natural binding properties to form it into a cake that can be cooked, then eaten either warm or cold.

Place the stock in a heavy saucepan and bring to a boil. Remove from the heat, stir in the couscous, and cover. Allow to sit for 5 minutes, until all of the liquid is absorbed. Stir in 1 tablespoon of the oil and the butter, tossing and fluffing up the grains with a fork. Cover the pot to keep warm.

Heat 1 tablespoon of the oil in a small pan. Add the scallions and garlic and sauté for 1 minute until soft. Add the cilantro and lemon juice. Remove the pan from the heat and fold in the crabmeat. Add the crab mixture to the couscous. Season with salt and pepper.

Fill a round cookie cutter (2 inches in diameter, 1 inch deep) with couscous to form a cake. Place the couscous cake on a baking sheet, pressing down on it so that it holds its round shape. Repeat, using all of the couscous mixture, to make between 8 and 10 cakes. Refrigerate until needed.

Heat 1 tablespoon of the oil in a large, heavy skillet. Quickly sauté 4 couscous cakes at a time, turning to brown for about 2 minutes on each side. Remove from the pan and drain on paper towels. Repeat with the remaining cakes, using more oil as needed. Serve with Cucumber Vinaigrette.

- 1½ cups Chicken Stock (see page 181) or Vegetable Stock (see page 180)
- 1 cup couscous
- Approximately ¼ cup virgin olive oil
- 1 tablespoon butter
- 4 scallions, greens and whites, finely minced
- 1 clove garlic, peeled and minced
- 1 tablespoon shredded fresh cilantro leaves
- 1 tablespoon lemon juice
- 8 ounces lump crabmeat, picked and cleaned
- Salt to taste
- Freshly ground black pepper to taste
- Cucumber Vinaigrette (recipe follows)

4 appetizer or 2 main course servings

cucumber vinaigrette

Place all of the ingredients in a blender and mix on high speed for 1 minute. Do not strain. Serve with the Crab and Scallion Couscous Cakes.

Makes 3 cups

- 2 large seedless cucumbers, peeled
- 1 clove garlic, peeled and minced
- 2 tablespoons fresh dill leaves
- ½ cup extra-virgin olive oil
- 2 tablespoons champagne vinegar (malt or cider vinegar may be substituted)
- 1 tablespoon freshly ground black pepper
- 1 teaspoon sugar
- Pinch of salt

Tabbouleh with Blueberries and Mint

THE NUTTINESS OF the tabbouleh is the perfect counterpoint to the natural sweetness of the blueberries and tanginess of the mint in this easy-to-make salad. If blueberries aren't available, substitute any soft berries.

- 1 cup #2 (medium-grind) bulgur wheat
- ½ pound fresh tomatoes, peeled, seeded, and diced
- ½ cucumber, peeled, seeded, and diced
- 4 scallions, whites and greens, minced
- 2 cups fresh blueberries, washed and stems removed
- 5 tablespoons fresh lemon juice
- ¼ cup olive oil
- ½ cup finely shredded fresh mint leaves
- 1 tablespoon finely chopped parsley
- ¼ teaspoon ground cumin
- ¼ teaspoon salt
- ¼ teaspoon freshly ground black pepper

Place the bulgur in a large mixing bowl. Bring 2 cups water to a rolling boil and add to the bulgur in the bowl. Stir well and allow to stand for 5 minutes. Turn the soaked wheat out onto a dry cloth and squeeze out any excess moisture. Return the wheat to the bowl and add the remaining ingredients, tossing gently to avoid damaging the blueberries.

Allow the mixture to stand and marinate for 2 hours. Serve at room temperature.

4 salad or side dish servings

Wheat Berries with Rice Wine Vinegar and Raspberries

THIS RECIPE CAN BE served as a side dish, as a salad, or, with a sprinkling of brown sugar on top, as a dessert.

- 1 cup whole, peeled wheat berries
- 2 tablespoons rice wine vinegar
- 1 tablespoon honey
- 1 pint raspberries, rinsed
- 4 lemon wedges
- 1 cup plain nonfat yogurt

Place the wheat berries in a fine sieve and rinse under cold running water for 1 minute.

Place in a mixing bowl, cover with cold water, and soak for 8 hours or overnight. Drain.

Place the drained wheat berries and 3 cups fresh water in a heavy, medium saucepan and bring to a boil over high heat. Reduce the heat, cover, and simmer until the wheat berries are tender but retain their crunch, about 1 hour. Remove the pan from the heat and allow to sit, covered, for 10 minutes. Drain the wheat berries and place in a mixing bowl.

Place the vinegar and honey in a medium saucepan and bring to a boil over high heat. Add the raspberries, stirring gently, and immediately remove the pan from the heat.

Carefully combine the raspberries with the wheat berries. Place on 4 serving plates and serve warm with the lemon and plain yogurt.

4 side dish, salad, or dessert servings

Sautéed Duck Breast with Wheat Berries and Apricots

IT IS THE CONTRAST of textures that makes this recipe special: The duck meat is firm yet tender; the apricot sauce is smooth and velvety; and the wheat berries are slightly crunchy.

If apricots are not available, try three peaches or Bartlett pears instead.

Place the wheat berries in a fine sieve and rinse under cold running water for 1 minute. Place in a mixing bowl, cover with water, and soak for 8 hours or overnight. Drain.

Place the drained wheat berries and 1¾ cups water in a heavy, medium saucepan and bring to a rolling boil. Reduce the heat to a simmer, cover, and cook for about 1 hour or until the grains are tender but retain their crunch. Remove the pan from the heat and allow to sit, covered, for 10 minutes. Spread out the berries on a baking sheet to cool quickly, then set aside.

Place the egg white in a mixing bowl and toss the duck strips in it. Roll each duck strip in the wheat berries, pressing lightly on each one to ensure that the berries adhere. (This process is best done by rolling each strip between your hands.) Repeat until all of the duck strips are covered. Set aside on the baking sheet.

- ½ cup whole, peeled wheat berries
- 1 egg white
- 4 4- to 6-ounce duck breasts, skinned and cut into ¼-inch strips
- 1 tablespoon canola oil
- 1 tablespoon sugar
- 1 teaspoon butter
- 1 clove garlic, peeled and minced
- 6 fresh apricots, peeled, seeded, and finely chopped
- ½ cup white wine

Heat the oil in a heavy skillet over medium heat. Add the duck strips and gently sauté for 30 seconds on each side. Drain the duck on kitchen towels and keep warm. Wipe the pan clean.

Add the sugar to the pan and cook over medium-high heat until a caramel forms and the sugar becomes the color of strong tea, approximately 10 minutes. Add the butter and garlic, stirring to make a candy. Add the chopped apricots and stir. Add the white wine, and, stirring continuously, bring to a boil and reduce by 50 percent.

Divide the duck strips among 4 serving plates. If desired, strain the sauce through a fine sieve. Serve the sauce alongside the duck.

4 main course servings

Bran Muffins

It is worth the effort to seek out Steen's syrup and Tate and Lyle's golden syrup for these muffins. Both brands have been around for generations and have retained their purity. To keep the syrups from sticking to the measuring spoon, warm the spoon first by running it under warm water.

In a large saucepan, bring the milk to a low boil. Place the bran in a large mixing bowl and slowly stir in the hot milk, stirring well to avoid lumps. Allow to sit and soften for 30 minutes.

Preheat the oven to 375° F. Lightly grease 12 4-ounce muffin cups with 1 tablespoon of the vegetable oil.

- *2 cups whole milk*
- *1 cup unprocessed coarse bran*
- *½ cup plus 1 tablespoon vegetable oil*
- *2 large eggs*
- *¼ cup honey*
- *2 tablespoons Steen's syrup (a thick cane syrup available at specialty food stores) or blackstrap molasses*
- *2 tablespoons Tate and Lyle's golden syrup (available at specialty food stores) or corn syrup*
- *1 cup all-purpose flour, sifted*
- *2 tablespoons baking powder*
- *Pinch of salt*
- *½ cup light brown sugar*
- *½ teaspoon cinnamon*
- *¼ cup raisins*

In a separate bowl, beat the eggs together, then add the remaining vegetable oil, the honey, and syrups to form a thick paste. Slowly add the flour, baking powder, and salt, mixing well to incorporate, then fold in the sugar, cinnamon, and raisins. Gradually stir in the bran and milk mixture until evenly incorporated.

Divide the batter among the greased muffin cups and bake for 20 to 25 minutes or until the muffins are light brown and slightly springy to the touch.

Remove from the oven and either cool on wire racks or serve immediately.

Makes 12 large muffins

Soda Bread

I LIKE TO EAT THIS traditional bread from Ireland with apples and cheese. The salt water that is brushed on the bread before baking adds flavor and helps to form a firm crust.

Preheat the oven to 425° F.

Sift the whole-wheat flour, 2 cups of the all-purpose flour, the baking soda, cream of tartar, and 2½ teaspoons of the salt into a large mixing bowl and blend together. Form a well in the center of the mixture and mix in the butter by hand, lifting and rubbing until the butter is incorporated into the dry ingredients. (It should be the consistency of coarse meal.) Add the buttermilk, mixing lightly with your hands until the dough pulls away from the sides of the bowl, dusting with additional flour if needed. Be careful not to overwork the dough, as this will make it tough.

- 2 cups whole-wheat flour
- 2½ cups all-purpose flour
- 1 tablespoon baking soda
- 1 tablespoon plus 1 teaspoon cream of tartar
- ¼ cup plus 2½ teaspoons salt
- 4 tablespoons (½ stick) unsalted butter, softened
- 2 cups buttermilk
- ½ cup water

Grease a baking sheet. Divide the dough in half and shape into 2 balls. With the palm of your hand, flatten each ball into a ½-inch-high disk, then place the disks on the greased baking sheet.

Blend the remaining salt and water together in a mixing cup. With a pastry brush, wash the top of the bread with the brine mixture, then dust heavily with the remaining ½ cup flour. With a sharp knife, cut a ¾-inch-deep cross into the top of each loaf.

Place the bread in the preheated oven and bake until the crust is a light golden brown and makes a hollow sound when tapped, about 25 to 30 minutes.

Remove the bread from the oven and transfer to a wire rack to cool slightly before serving.

Makes 2 loaves

Plum Tart

Use this tart crust not only for plums but also for other firm fruits, such as pears, apricots, peaches, and nectarines. I use Tate and Lyle's golden syrup as it adds a natural sweetness that contrasts with the tartness of the plums.

Place the flours, bran, and salt in the bowl of a mixer fitted with a dough hook or paddle attachment or place the ingredients in an ordinary mixing bowl.

In a separate medium mixing bowl, dissolve the yeast in the buttermilk and syrup. After the yeast has dissolved (after about 5 to 7 minutes), pour the mixture into the bowl with the dry ingredients. Mix on low speed until the dough comes together, about 4 minutes, or mix by hand until the mixture comes together into a dough, pulling away from the sides of the bowl. Remove the bowl from the machine and cover with a damp cloth. Allow to rest in a warm, draft-free place for 30 minutes.

Place the halved plums on a cutting board and carefully slice each half into thirds lengthwise, being careful not to cut all the way through (the slices should still be joined together).

- *½ cup unbleached all-purpose flour*
- *½ cup whole-wheat flour*
- *2½ tablespoons unprocessed coarse bran*
- *1 teaspoon salt*
- *1 package active dry yeast*
- *½ cup buttermilk*
- *¼ cup Tate and Lyle's golden syrup (available at specialty food stores) or corn syrup*
- *18 fresh plums, pitted and halved*
- *½ cup honey*
- *1 teaspoon butter*
- *½ cup apricot preserves*

Warm the honey in a small saucepan over low heat and cover to keep warm.

Grease a small (8-inch-by-10-inch) baking sheet with the butter. Place the dough on a lightly floured surface and roll into an 8-inch-by-10-inch rectangle, ¼ inch thick, then place on the baking sheet so that it covers the entire sheet. Prick holes into the dough with a fork, then spread on the apricot preserves. Fan the plums open in the palm of your hand, then place in a line across the dough. Repeat the procedure, overlapping each line, so that the entire surface of the dough is covered.

Brush the plums lightly with the warm honey, then allow the tart to rest for 30 minutes in a warm place.

Preheat the oven to 350° F.

Bake the tart for 30 to 45 minutes or until the plums are tender and cooked. Remove the tart from the oven and brush again with the warm honey. Allow the tart to cool slightly before cutting. The tart can be served either hot or at room temperature.

6 to 8 servings

Multi-Grain Bread

BREADS OF THIS NATURE are becoming increasingly popular as people demand more fiber in their diets and begin to appreciate the great flavor and texture that different grains offer. Experiment with your own grain blends and also try adding nuts, such as pecans, walnuts, or hazelnuts.

Place the flours, grains, and salt in the bowl of a mixer fitted with a dough hook or paddle or in an ordinary mixing bowl.

Place the water, yeast, and sugar in a separate bowl and stir until the yeast has dissolved, about 5 minutes.

Pour the yeast mixture into the flour mixture and mix on low speed until well combined, about 5 minutes. (Alternatively, fold the yeast mixture into the flour mixture and mix well by hand.) Cover the bowl with a damp cloth and put in a draft-free, warm place (such as beside the oven) for 45 minutes or until the dough has doubled in volume.

Punch the dough down with your hands (to push the gasses out) and allow to rest for another 15 minutes. Form the dough into a ball, place in the bowl again, and cover with a damp cloth. Allow to rest for 5 minutes.

Grease a baking sheet with the sesame and olive oils.

- ⅓ cup whole-wheat flour
- 1 cup bread flour
- ¾ cup six-grain flour (see Note)
- ¼ cup nine-grain blend (see Note)
- 1 tablespoon millet
- 1 teaspoon black sesame seeds
- 1 teaspoon salt

- ½ cup tepid water
- 1 package active dry yeast
- 1 teaspoon sugar
- 1 tablespoon sesame oil
- 2 tablespoons virgin olive oil
- 1 tablespoon each cornmeal, millet, rolled oats, and sesame seeds

Remove the ball of dough from the bowl and flatten on a lightly floured surface with the palm of your hand. Fold one edge into the center, press, and roll into a torpedo shape. Place the dough on the greased pan with the seam on the bottom. Place the pan in a warm place for 30 to 40 minutes, or until the dough has doubled in volume.

Preheat the oven to 450° F.

Sprinkle the top of the loaf with the cornmeal, millet, rolled oats, and sesame seeds. Bake for 30 to 40 minutes or until golden brown. Remove the bread from the pan and allow to cool on a wire rack.

Note: If you are unable to find either six-grain flour or nine-grain blend, you can mix your own in equal parts or to taste for the total amount needed in the recipe:

Six-grain flour—any combination of six of the following: wheat flour, crushed rye, rye flour, barley, oatmeal, cornmeal, linseed, millet, and sesame seed.

Nine-grain blend—coarse ground cereal mix of red wheat, white wheat, corn, barley, oats, millet, flax, bran, and rye.

Makes one 1½-pound loaf

BUCKWHEAT

Not a true grain, buckwheat is the fruit of a leafy plant related to rhubarb and garden sorrel; it is closer to a complete protein than any of the true grains. It probably originated in Central Asia around the tenth century B.C., but didn't reach Europe until well into the Middle Ages. Dutch and German colonists carried buckwheat to the New World, where it has never reached its potential as a food source. A featured ingredient in many Eastern European dishes, such as kasha varnishkes (roasted buckwheat groats with bowtie noodles), pierogi (noodle dumplings), and stuffed cabbage, it is also used to make bread in China.

Most commonly available in the United States are roasted, hulled buckwheat kernels, which have a strong, toasted nut taste and are usually labeled as buckwheat groats or kasha. Much milder in flavor and a good substitute for white or brown rice are unroasted (or white), hulled buckwheat kernels. Finely ground unroasted groats, which become soft and creamy as they cook, are sold as buckwheat cereal or cream of buckwheat. Buckwheat flour is used to make Japanese soba noodles, American flapjacks, and Russian blini (small, thin pancakes served with sour cream and caviar or smoked salmon). An additional and extraordinary product of this grain is buckwheat honey.

Kasha with Shrimp, Lemon, and Rosemary

- 2 tablespoons canola oil
- 1 large yellow onion, peeled and finely diced
- 1 clove garlic, peeled and minced
- 1 tablespoon fresh lemon zest
- ¼ teaspoon fresh rosemary leaves, minced
- 1 cup kasha (roasted buckwheat groats)
- 2 large eggs, beaten well
- 2 cups boiling water
- 1 cup raw, peeled baby (small) shrimp
- Salt and pepper

Heat the oil in a large, heavy sauté pan over medium-high heat. Add the onion and sauté until light brown, about 5 minutes. Add the garlic, lemon zest, and rosemary, and continue cooking for 1 minute. Remove the mixture from the pan to a bowl and cover to keep warm.

In a separate bowl, mix together the kasha and eggs. Return the pan to medium heat and add the kasha-egg mixture. Cook, stirring continuously, until the kasha grains are coated with egg and separate, about 2 minutes. Slowly add the boiling water, ¼ cup at a time, until all of the water is incorporated.

Return the onion mixture to the pan, bring to a simmer, cover, and cook for about 20 to 25 minutes, stirring from time to time. Add the shrimp to the pan and cook for 3 to 4 minutes. Remove the pan from the heat, allow to stand 5 minutes, then season with salt and pepper and serve.

4 appetizer or side dish servings

Pink Peppercorn Buckwheat Cakes and Smoked Sturgeon with Sour Cream and Salmon Caviar Topping

Combine the water, yeast, and sugar in a mixing bowl and stir until the yeast has dissolved, about 5 minutes. (Note that yeast will bubble as it ferments.)

In a separate, large bowl, combine the buckwheat and all-purpose flours, peppercorns, and salt. Gradually mix in the hot milk and fermenting yeast. Fold in the egg yolks. Cover the bowl with a clean towel and place in a warm, draft-free spot (such as beside the stove) until the batter has doubled in volume, about 1½ hours.

In a separate bowl, beat the egg whites until stiff. After the batter has doubled in volume, using a soft rubber spatula, gently fold in the egg whites, turning the bowl in one direction and at the same time turning the spatula in the other.

- ½ cup tepid water
- 1 package active dry yeast
- ¼ cup sugar
- 1 cup buckwheat flour
- 1 cup all-purpose flour
- ½ tablespoon crushed pink peppercorns
- ½ teaspoon salt
- 2 cups hot milk
- 3 eggs, separated
- 2 tablespoons vegetable oil
- ½ cup very thinly sliced smoked sturgeon
- Sour Cream and Salmon Caviar Topping (recipe follows)

Heat a small amount of oil in a 6-inch nonstick skillet over medium heat. Using a ¼-cup ladle, pour a pool of batter into the center of the pan. As the cake cooks, bubbles will begin to form on the top; when the bubbles become evident sprinkle a little shredded sturgeon into the batter. Turn the cake over and cook for another 30 seconds or until a light golden brown on the second side. Repeat with the remaining batter and sturgeon, keeping the cooked cakes warm.

Serve Buckwheat Cakes immediately with Sour Cream and Salmon Caviar Topping.

Makes 24 cakes / 6 appetizer or 4 main course servings

sour cream and salmon caviar topping

THE SEPARATED hard-boiled eggs for this recipe are sieved before they are added to the cream mixture in order to create the traditional caviar garnish.

In a mixing bowl, combine

- 1 cup sour cream
- ¼ red Bermuda onion, minced
- 2 hard-boiled eggs, yolks and whites separated and sieved
- 1 teaspoon chopped parsley
- ¼ cup salmon caviar or caviar variety of choice

all of the ingredients except the caviar. Transfer to a decorative serving bowl and sprinkle the caviar on top. Serve as an accompaniment to Pink Peppercorn Buckwheat Cakes.

QUINOA

Quinoa (pronounced KEEN-wah) is said to have been named by the Spanish conquistador Francisco Pizzaro who, in the sixteenth century, upon seeing in the Peruvian Andes the tall stalks and beautiful blossoms of the plant, exclaimed, "Quimera," or "Fantastic." Soon after, however, Pizzaro banned the cultivation of quinoa, which was considered sacred by the Incas and used in their religious ceremonies, ordering that the Incas become more "civilized" and grow barley instead.

Though known as a "supergrain" in modern society and "the mother grain" among the Incas, quinoa is not really a grain. This nutritional powerhouse—it is high in protein and iron, among other nutrients—belongs to the same family as spinach. Ranging in color from buff to russet to black, quinoa seeds are flat, pointed ovals. When cooked, the seed's external germ forms a tiny "tail" at one end and its texture becomes light, springy, and crunchy. The flavor of quinoa is mildly sweet and earthy.

Because quinoa grains are protected from insects, birds, and the radiation of high-altitude sun by a bitter, soapy natural coating called saponin—which may explain this grain's survival over thousands of years— they need to be washed before cooking and eating. Though this is usually taken care of by processors before quinoa reaches grocery store shelves, it is a good idea to rinse the grains again before cooking to remove any residue.

Quinoa

QUINOA IS DELICIOUS tossed with vegetables or mixed with corn or other grains. Any mild herb, such as fresh chervil or basil, may be substituted for the mint in this recipe.

> - 1 cup quinoa
> - 2 cups Chicken Stock (see page 181)
> - 1 large clove garlic, peeled and minced
> - 1 medium bay leaf
> - 4 white peppercorns
> - 2 star anise seed pods
> - Pinch of salt
> - 1 tablespoon olive oil
> - 1 tablespoon chopped fresh mint leaves

Place the quinoa in a fine sieve and rinse under cold running water for about 5 minutes, stirring occasionally, until the water runs clear. (The longer you rinse the grain, the milder in flavor it will become.) Drain.

Place the stock, garlic, bay leaf, peppercorns, star anise, and salt in a heavy saucepan and bring to a boil over medium-high heat. Add the quinoa and return to a boil. Reduce the heat and simmer until the quinoa looks glassy and translucent (indicating it is cooked through), about 15 minutes. Remove from the heat. Let the quinoa stand for 5 minutes, then stir in the oil and mint with a fork, fluffing up the grains as you toss lightly.

Makes 3½ cups / 4 side dish servings

Quinoa with Peppered Rabbit Loin

IF WILD RABBIT—which is more flavorful than farm-raised rabbit—is available, definitely use it in this recipe.

> - 3½ cups cooked Quinoa (see left), covered and kept warm while preparing the rabbit
> - 8 2- to 3-ounce rabbit loins
> - ½ teaspoon herbes de Provence (dried herb mixture sold at specialty food stores)
> - 1 tablespoon freshly ground black pepper
> - Pinch of salt
> - ¼ cup virgin olive oil

Clean the rabbit loins by carefully cutting away any sinew and fat that may surround the meat.

In a flat dish, combine the herbes de Provence, pepper, and salt. Roll each loin in the seasonings so that the mixture adheres to the surface, lightly pressing the seasonings into the rabbit by rolling the meat between your hands. Repeat with each loin and set aside.

Place a heavy sauté pan over high heat and add the oil. Sauté each loin on each side for about 2 minutes, until golden brown. Remove the meat from the pan and drain on kitchen towels, which will also give the meat a chance to rest (and become more tender). Divide the rabbit loins and quinoa among 4 servings plates.

4 main course servings

Baby Artichokes Stuffed with Quinoa and Nut Dressing

FOR ADDED FLAVOR, I like to serve this earthy appetizer with a roasted garlic vinaigrette: Combine 1 tablespoon Roasted Garlic Purée (see page 181) with 2 tablespoons olive oil, 1 tablespoon malt or cider vinegar, 1 finely chopped shallot, 1 teaspoon chopped fresh parsley, and salt and pepper.

artichokes

Remove any tough outer leaves from the artichokes and cut each across the top to remove any small spiky tips.

Heat ¼ cup of the olive oil in a heavy pot over medium-high heat. Add the onion, garlic, red pepper, and bay leaf, and sauté until the onion is soft, about 3 minutes. Add the artichokes to the pot and sauté for 1 minute, stirring constantly. Add the white wine, chicken stock, lemon juice, salt, and pepper to the pot. Lower the heat, cover, and simmer for about 10 minutes, until the artichokes are tender. Remove the pot from the heat, uncover, and allow to cool for about 15 minutes.

Drain the artichokes in a colander, then squeeze very gently to remove any remaining liquid. Gently open the center of each artichoke and stuff it with 1 tablespoon of the Quinoa and Nut Dressing. Repeat with each artichoke, placing them on a serving platter as you finish. Sprinkle the stuffed artichokes with the Parmesan cheese and drizzle with the remaining ¼ cup olive oil. Serve at room temperature.

6 appetizer servings

- *24 baby artichokes, washed and bottom stems trimmed*
- *½ cup virgin olive oil*
- *½ cup peeled and finely diced yellow onion*
- *1 clove garlic, peeled*
- *1 teaspoon red pepper flakes*
- *1 bay leaf*
- *1½ cups white wine*
- *2½ cups Chicken Stock (see page 181)*
- *½ cup fresh lemon juice*
- *Salt to taste*
- *Freshly ground black pepper to taste*
- *Quinoa and Nut Dressing (recipe follows)*
- *½ cup freshly grated Parmesan cheese*

quinoa and nut dressing

- *1½ cups cooked Quinoa (see page 111)*
- *2 tablespoons walnuts or pecans, finely chopped*
- *2 tablespoons hazelnuts, finely chopped*
- *2 tablespoons pistachio nuts, finely chopped*
- *2 tablespoons minced fresh mint leaves*
- *⅓ cup extra-virgin olive oil*
- *3 tablespoons fresh lemon juice*
- *1 teaspoon freshly ground black pepper*

Combine all of the ingredients in a mixing bowl and let stand at room temperature while preparing the artichokes.

Grilled Chicken with Quinoa
and Sautéed Fennel

Place the chicken in a large bowl or baking dish.

Combine the remaining ingredients through the white wine in a saucepan and heat quickly to just below a boil. Remove from the heat and pour over the chicken. Allow the chicken to marinate for at least 2 hours at room temperature or in the refrigerator overnight.

- 4 large chicken breasts or 1 whole chicken, split down the back and quartered
- 4 cloves garlic, peeled and minced
- 1 tablespoon crushed black peppercorns
- Pinch of red pepper flakes
- Pinch of salt
- Pinch of dried thyme
- Pinch of dried rosemary
- Pinch of lavender seeds (optional)
- ½ cup virgin olive oil
- 1 cup dry white wine
- 3½ cups cooked Quinoa (see page 111), covered and kept warm while preparing the chicken
- Sautéed Fennel (recipe follows)

Heat a grill until the coals turn white. Place the chicken on the grill and cook, basting occasionally with the marinade, until the chicken begins to brown, about 20 minutes per side.

When done, place the chicken on top of the warm quinoa and serve with Sautéed Fennel on the side.

4 main course servings

sautéed fennel

Wash the fennel well and remove any discolored outer leaves. With a sharp knife, split each bulb into four pieces lengthwise. Remove as much of the tough roots as possible without losing any leaves.

- 4 small bulbs fennel (the heart of 1 bunch of celery may be substituted)
- 2 tablespoons virgin olive oil
- 2 cups Chicken Stock (see page 181)
- 4 sprigs fresh thyme
- Salt to taste
- Freshly ground black pepper to taste

Heat the oil in a large skillet over medium-high heat. Place the fennel, flat side down, in the oil and sauté for about

2 minutes. Add the stock, thyme, and a pinch of salt, and bring to a boil. Reduce the heat to a simmer, cover, and cook for about 20 minutes. The fennel should remain firm. Remove the pan from the heat, season the fennel with pepper, and serve with its cooking liquid with the Grilled Chicken and Quinoa.

OATS

Oats have probably been cultivated since the dawn of agriculture but have throughout history nourished many more animals, especially horses, than humans. Among humans, the biggest oat eaters have always been the Celts, and in particular the Scots. In fact, an old Scottish cookbook dubs oats "one of the sweetest grains to cook with," and in the nineteenth century, Scottish parents observed Oatmeal Monday by delivering to their sons who were studying at university a sack of oats, meant to keep them healthy throughout the approaching winter term.

The most common form in which to eat oats is, of course, oatmeal (otherwise known as porridge, gruel, or mush). A good source of protein, B vitamins, calcium, unsaturated fats, and fiber (oats are one of the few grains from which the bran and germ are not removed during processing), oats can also play a significant role in other dishes, such as stuffings, all sorts of baked goods, and soups.

Among the numerous forms in which oats are available are oat groats (whole oat kernels from which only the inedible outer hull has been removed); rolled oats (oat kernels that have been heated and flattened so that they will cook more quickly—these make a great substitute for bread crumbs when cooking fish); steel-cut oats, also known as Scottish or Irish oats (oats kernels that have been sliced lengthwise); and oat bran (the outer layer of oat kernels).

Oatmeal

OATMEAL IS PROBABLY the most underrated breakfast food, yet for me it is the best.

> • 1⅓ cups rolled oats
> • 2 cups skim milk
> • 1 cup water
> • Pinch of salt (optional)
> • Sliced fresh fruit, berries, cream, brown sugar, or other topping (optional)

In a heavy saucepan, combine the rolled oats, skim milk, water, and salt (if using) and slowly bring to a boil, stirring continuously and watching carefully as oatmeal burns quickly. Reduce the heat to a simmer and cook for about 4 minutes, continuing to stir. Remove the pan from the heat, cover, and let stand for a few minutes before serving.

Spoon into bowls and, if desired, add one or more toppings.

2 servings

Atholl Brose

THIS DRINK was originated by the Earl of Atholl in 1475. Atholl filled the Earl of Ross's well with it, making Ross's men so drunk that he was able to capture Ross's castle. Today Atholl Brose is traditionally served in Scotland on New Year's Eve to the first guests crossing the threshold of the host's home, hence its other name, First Footing.

> • 3 tablespoons rolled oats
> • 2 tablespoons heather honey (other flavors of honey may be substituted)
> • 1 quart Scotch whiskey

Place the oatmeal in a mixing bowl and add just enough cold water to make a thin paste. Allow the mixture to stand for about 1 hour, then strain through a fine sieve into a large clean bowl, pressing the oatmeal against the sieve with the back of a spoon to release the liquid. Discard the oatmeal.

Mix the oatmeal liquid with the honey, then add the Scotch. Rebottle the liquid and shake well before serving. Serve either straight up or with a mixer.

Makes 1 quart

AMARANTH

Amaranth, though considered a grain, is actually a plant related to both the tumbleweed of the American southwest and the garden weed known as pigweed. Like other non-true grains (such as quinoa and buckwheat), it contains lysine, an amino acid missing from most grains that controls protein absorption in the body. Amaranth is also rich in iron (only quinoa exceeds it in iron content), calcium—1⅓ cups cooked amaranth has as much calcium as ½ cup milk— folacin, and magnesium.

Amaranth grains are very small—about the size of poppy seeds—range in color from ivory to dark purple (though most amaranth on the market is pale yellow), and boast a chewy texture and nutty, slightly peppery flavor that is sometimes compared to toasted sesame seeds. Steamed amaranth seeds have a particularly satisfying mouth texture—you can feel the individual grains in your mouth. The seeds also pop like corn when dry-fried in a pan.

Until the sixteenth century, when the Spanish explorers arrived in Mexico, amaranth was a key ingredient in the Aztec diet and played an important role in religious rituals, including idolatrous ceremonies. Offended by these ceremonies—and what he considered an affront to Christianity—the Spanish conquistador Cortés had all of the amaranth fields burned and deemed possession or cultivation of the grain a serious crime (the punishment was the chopping off of both hands). The effect of these actions, according to historians, was the starvation of the Aztecs into submission and the destruction of the Aztec culture.

Amaranth Pear Pie

THIS RECIPE YIELDS two pies. If only one pie is desired, I suggest making both crusts (freezing the extra one) and halfing the pear filling. The amaranth flour in the crust contributes an appealing nutty flavor.

- 1 cup amaranth flour
- 1 cup unbleached all-purpose flour
- 1½ cups ground hazelnuts
- 1 teaspoon salt
- 1 stick (4 ounces) butter
- ½ cup sugar
- 4 whole eggs
- ¼ cup lowfat buttermilk
- Juice of 3 lemons
- 18 ripe Anjou pears
- 1 cup brown sugar
- 1 tablespoon butter or vegetable oil

Combine the amaranth and all-purpose flours, 1 cup of the ground hazelnuts, and the salt in a mixing bowl. Set aside.

Place the butter and sugar in the large bowl of a mixer fitted with a paddle attachment and cream for 5 minutes. With the mixer on low speed, add 3 of the eggs and the buttermilk to the creamed butter. Slowly incorporate the dry ingredients and mix until a dough just forms, being careful not to overmix. Wrap the dough in plastic wrap and allow to rest for at least 30 minutes.

Place the lemon juice in a large mixing bowl. Peel and core the pears, then cut each one lengthwise into 6 even slices. Add the pear slices to the mixing bowl with the lemon juice, tossing to coat. Sprinkle the brown sugar over the pears and mix well, being careful not to break the slices. Set aside.

Preheat the oven to 375° F.

Beat the remaining egg in a small dish and set aside.

Grease 2 10-inch pie pans with the 1 tablespoon butter or

vegetable oil. Divide the dough into 4 equal parts. On a lightly floured surface, roll out one ball of dough into a 10-inch circle, ¼ inch thick. Line one pie pan with the dough, leaving a ¼-inch overhang. Place half the pear mixture on the dough, being careful not to get any pear on the side of the pan. Roll out the second ball of dough to a ¼-inch thickness and top the pear filling with this dough, folding the overhanging edge of the first dough over that of the second to seal. Crimp the edge of the pie with a fork to completely seal the filling. Cut slits into the top crust of the pie and brush the crust with half the beaten egg. Sprinkle the top crust with ¼ cup of the remaining ground hazelnuts. Set aside and assemble the second pie in the same manner.

Place the pies in the preheated oven and bake for 30 to 40 minutes or until the top crusts are golden brown. Remove from the oven and allow to cool 30 minutes before cutting. Serve either warm or at room temperature.

Makes 2 10-inch pies

RYE

Rye wasn't widely used as a food source until the Middle Ages, when a European farmer—probably exhausted by the arduous task of continuously pulling it out like a weed—decided to harvest it with his wheat. Hardy and able to withstand colder and wetter climates than many other grains, rye became the principle grain in the breads of Britian, Scandinavia, Russia, Germany, and much of Eastern Europe. It was brought to America by the Dutch and Germans in the seventeenth century, though in this country it was never exploited as a food source; rather, it was turned into rye whiskey by Western cowboys. Today twenty-five percent of the annual rye crop in the United States is transformed into human food, while the remaining seventy-five percent is used to make rye whiskey, other spirits, and animal feed.

The most common form of rye in United States food markets is rye flour, which comes in several different varieties, from light, also known as white (from which most of the bran has been removed), to medium, to dark, to pumpernickel (which has the strongest flavor and usually the most bran). Because there are no industry-wide standards, the amount of bran left in a particular kind of rye flour varies from brand to brand. Rye produces very little gluten, the protein that gives dough strength and elasticity, so it must be mixed with white or whole wheat flour—approximately 30 percent rye to 70 percent wheat flour—in order to make rye bread.

Other forms of rye that are used in cooking include:

Whole rye berries (kernels or groats): whole grains with outer hulls removed. To shorten the lengthy time required to cook these berries (½ cup unsoaked berries in 1½ cups liquid will take close to 2 hours), soak them in cold water in the refrigerator overnight; then, to conserve nutrients, cook the berries in the soaking liquid.

Rye flakes or rolled rye: rye berries that are heated, then pressed with a steel roller. Rye flakes look like rolled oats but are thicker. They can be used to make a hot breakfast cereal or can be mixed into bread or other baked goods.

Rye grits: Whole rye berries ground into small pieces. Use as a cereal or mix with other grains to make bread.

Rye Berries with Shredded Apples and Raspberries

THE NATURAL ACIDITY of the rye is enhanced by the fruit, yet tempered by the sugar. This dish is great with grilled fish or poultry.

- 1 cup whole rye berries
- 3½ cups water
- 1 tablespoon sugar
- 1 tablespoon malt vinegar (champagne or cider vinegar may be substituted)
- ½ teaspoon crushed pink peppercorns
- 1 Granny Smith apple, peeled, cored, and shredded or grated
- 1 pint fresh raspberries

Spread the rye out on a work surface and pick over to remove any grains that are discolored or appear deformed. Place the rye in a fine sieve and rinse under cold running water for 2 minutes.

Place the rye and water in a heavy, medium saucepan and bring to a rolling boil. Reduce the heat, cover, and simmer for about 1 hour or until the grains are tender but retain their crunch. Remove the pan from the heat and allow to sit, covered, for 10 minutes. Pour the grains into a mixing bowl and allow to cool, about 5 minutes, then add the sugar, vinegar, and peppercorns. Fold in the shredded apple, mixing well, then immediately before serving add the raspberries.

4 to 6 side dish servings

Rice and Pasta

RICE

Rice probably originated in India or China about 3000 B.C., but spread rapidly because it grew easily—all it needs is plenty of water—and because of its adaptability to various climates. Rice paddies now circle the globe, from the Far East to Africa and from Europe to the Americas.

Today there are thousands of rice varieties, providing twenty-five to eighty percent of the calories in the daily diet of half the world's population. It is a vital component in meals of Asia, Africa, South America, and parts of North America and Europe. Americans still eat primarily long-grain white rice but have begun in the last decade or so to broaden their rice horizons. Following are some of the world's favorite types:

Arborio rice: a short-grained rice that grows in the fertile, wet Po Valley in the Piedmont region of Italy. Because it is sheathed in both a soft starch that dissolves in cooking and a harder starch that stays firm when cooked, it is ideally suited for making risotto, the Italian rice specialty in which the cooked rice grains must be at once both creamy and firm.

Basmati rice: a slightly sweet and nutty, long-grained rice that is cultivated in the foothills of the Himalayas. It is the only rice that expands lengthwise as it cooks. Calmati and Texmati are similar rices grown in the United States.

Jasmine rice: a fragrant, soft, long-grained white rice from Thailand.

Short-grain rice: round or oval grains with a high percentage of amylopectin, the starch that makes rices grains cling to one another; favored in Japan and also for use in risottos.

Glutinous, sticky, waxy, or sweet rice: the stickiest short-grained rice available; used throughout much of Asia to make sweet, chewy cakes and other desserts.

Brown rice: rice from which the bran has not been removed.

Red rice: a short-grain brown rice with a reddish tinge and a flavor reminiscent of wild mushrooms.

PAGE 122 *Clockwise from top:* Arborio rice, Basmati rice, wild rice, Japanese short-grain rice, buckwheat pasta

PAGE 123 *Clockwise from top left:* red rice, brown rice, semolina pasta

Saffron Pilaf with Shredded Lamb and Basil

THE COMBINATION OF basil and saffron provides a wonderful contrast to the flavor and texture of the lamb in this recipe.

Preheat the oven to 375° F.

Heat the oil over medium heat in a large, heavy saucepan. Add the saffron and sauté for 1 minute, stirring constantly. (As the saffron cooks, it will color the oil a light yellow.) Add the onion, garlic, bay leaf, cardamom, and clove to the pan and sauté for 2 minutes. Add the rice to the pan and sauté for 2 additional minutes, stirring constantly. Add the stock and wine and bring to a boil. Cover and place in the oven to cook for about 15 to 17 minutes, until the liquid is absorbed. Remove from the oven and keep warm.

- 3 tablespoons olive oil
- 12 saffron threads
- 1 large yellow onion, peeled and finely chopped
- 1 clove garlic, peeled and minced
- 1 medium bay leaf
- 2 cardamom seeds, hulled and crushed
- 1 clove
- 1½ cups Basmati rice
- 2 cups hot Chicken Stock (see page 181)
- 1 cup dry white wine
- Salt to taste
- Freshly ground black pepper to taste
- Shredded Lamb and Basil (recipe follows)

4 main course servings

shredded lamb and basil

SHREDDING LAMB tenderizes it and gives it a much better texture than grinding.

Combine the lamb, garlic, basil, oil, salt, and pepper in a bowl. Mix well and divide into 4 equal parts. Heat a large, heavy nonstick frying pan to just below smoking. Add 1 portion of lamb and press down into the pan as it cooks so that the meat forms a cake across the diameter of the pan. Sear for 1 minute until brown. Carefully turn with a spatula and sear on the other side. Remove and drain on a clean kitchen towel. Repeat with the other 3 portions.

Place the lamb cakes on 4 plates and serve with Saffron Pilaf.

Note: The shredding is best done by your butcher. The sinew and fat need to be removed before shredding.

- 1 pound lamb leg, finely shredded (see Note)
- 1 tablespoon minced garlic
- 1 tablespoon minced fresh basil leaves
- 1 tablespoon olive oil
- Salt to taste
- Freshly ground black pepper to taste

Braised Basmati Rice with Lobster, Oven-Dried Tomatoes, and Yogurt Mint Sauce

IF YOU PREFER not to use lobster in this dish, substitute shrimp, crawfish tails, or lump crabmeat. Do not substitute any other kind of rice for the Basmati.

- 2 tablespoons canola oil
- ½ large white onion, peeled and finely chopped
- 1 clove garlic, minced
- 1 medium bay leaf
- 1 clove
- 4 cardamom pods, husked and ground
- 1 cup Basmati rice
- ½ teaspoon ground turmeric
- 2 cups Chicken Stock (see page 181)
- Salt to taste
- Freshly ground black pepper to taste
- 1 pound cooked lobster meat, diced
- ¼ cup chopped fresh cilantro leaves
- 8 Oven-Dried Tomatoes (recipe follows)
- Yogurt Mint Sauce (recipe follows)

Preheat the oven to 375° F.

In a large, heavy saucepan, heat the oil over medium heat. Add the onion, garlic, bay leaf, clove, and cardamom, and sauté for 3 minutes, or until the onion is soft. Add the rice and sauté for 2 minutes, stirring constantly. Add the turmeric, stirring well, then the chicken stock, salt, and pepper. Bring to a boil, then remove from the heat. Cover the pan and cook in the oven for 15 to 17 minutes, until the liquid is absorbed.

Remove the rice from the oven and fluff with a fork. Fold in the lobster and cilantro, then divide among 4 serving plates, garnishing each with the Oven-Dried Tomatoes. Pass the Yogurt Mint Sauce at the table.

4 appetizer servings

oven-dried tomatoes

THE DRYING PROCESS intensifies the natural sweetness of tomatoes. Use them to add flavor to pasta dishes, tabbouleh, and couscous.

> • 8 large Italian plum tomatoes, washed and dried
> • 1 teaspoon sugar
> • 1 teaspoon salt

Preheat the oven to its lowest temperature, approximately 200° F.

Slice the tomatoes lengthwise into quarters and lay on a baking sheet lined with parchment paper, seed-side up. Mix the sugar and salt together in a small bowl and sprinkle evenly over the tomatoes.

Place the baking sheet in the oven and allow the tomatoes to dry for at least 12 and up to 24 hours.

Remove the tomatoes from the oven and cool. Store in an airtight container until ready to use, up to 2 to 3 weeks. For longer storage, submerge the tomatoes in olive oil, cover, and refrigerate.

yogurt mint sauce

> • 1 cup loosely packed mint leaves, finely chopped
> • 1 teaspoon sugar
> • 1 cup plain yogurt

Mix the mint leaves and sugar together in a small bowl, then stir into the yogurt. Serve in a small decorative bowl as an accompaniment to the Braised Basmati Rice with Lobster and the Oven-Dried Tomatoes.

Wasabi-Sesame Rice Cakes with Mascarpone Dip

SHORT-GRAIN JAPANESE RICE has a natural glutinous quality. Seeing Japanese chefs form this rice into balls for sushi inspired me to flatten the balls into cakes.

I've used Mascarpone cheese here because it mellows the sharp flavor of the wasabi and marries it with the natural sweetness of the rice.

- 1½ cups short-grain Japanese rice
- ¼ cup rice wine vinegar
- ¾ cup sugar
- 1 cup sesame seeds
- 1 tablespoon wasabi powder (Japanese dried horseradish powder available at Asian or other specialty food stores)
- 2 tablespoons sesame oil
- Mascarpone Dip (recipe follows)

Place the rice in a bowl, cover with cold water, and allow to soak for 10 minutes. Place the rice in a colander and rinse under cold running water for 5 minutes or until the water runs clear. Drain.

Place the rice and 1¾ cups cold water in a heavy stockpot and cover. Slowly bring to a boil, then reduce to a simmer for 10 minutes. Remove the pot from the heat and allow to stand for 30 minutes—do not stir or remove the lid during this time.

In a small pan, heat the vinegar and sugar over medium-high heat, stirring constantly, until the sugar dissolves.

Pour the rice into a very large mixing bowl and spoon in the sugared vinegar, mixing well with a flat wooden spoon or spatula until the vinegar is evenly distributed and the rice takes on a sheen. Keep lifting the rice with the spoon until it is cool enough to handle with your hands, fanning it with a magazine or hand-held fan to speed the process, if you wish.

Divide the rice mixture into 12 equal portions. Form each portion into a ball, then press tightly between your hands to form a disk about $3\frac{1}{2}$ to 4 inches in diameter. Set the disks aside on a clean dish.

Combine the sesame seeds and wasabi powder in a small bowl, then transfer to a flat dish. Press each rice disk lightly into the powder mixture, coating each side evenly.

Heat the oil in a heavy skillet over medium-high heat. Sauté the cakes until golden brown on both sides, about 2 to 3 minutes per side. Remove from the pan and drain on paper towels. Serve immediately with the Mascarpone Dip.

6 appetizer or 2 main course servings

mascarpone dip

- 2 cups Mascarpone cheese
- 2 tablespoons wasabi powder
- 1 tablespoon honey

Combine all of the ingredients in a blender set on medium-high for 1 minute. Serve at room temperature with the Wasabi-Sesame Rice Cakes.

Makes 2 cups

Red Rice with Diced Bananas, Curried Cauliflower, and Mango Shake

THIS DISH IS derived from the Indian potato-cauliflower dish called Aloo Gobi, except I replace the potato with banana.

- 2 cups red rice (Basmati rice may be substituted)
- 5 cups Chicken Stock (see page 181)
- 1 tablespoon vegetable oil
- 1 large yellow onion, diced
- 1 clove garlic, minced
- 1 medium bay leaf
- 1 teaspoon garam masala (Indian spice mixture available at Asian or other specialty food stores)
- 2 ripe red bananas (firm yellow bananas may be substituted), peeled and chopped into small pieces
- Salt to taste
- Freshly ground black pepper to taste
- Curried Cauliflower (recipe follows on page 132)
- Mango Shake (recipe follows on page 132)

Place the rice in a fine sieve and rinse under cold running water for 5 minutes. Drain.

Heat the chicken stock to a low boil, cover, and set aside. Heat the oil over high heat in a large, heavy pot. Add the onion, garlic, and bay leaf, and sauté for 5 minutes or until the onion is translucent. Add the rice and sauté for 1 minute. Add the garam masala, stirring well, and sauté for 1 minute. Add the hot chicken stock, lower the heat, cover, and simmer for 15 to 20 minutes or until the rice has absorbed all of the liquid. Remove the pan from the heat and remove the bay leaf. Fold in the chopped bananas. Season with salt and pepper and serve with Curried Cauliflower and Mango Shake.

4 main course servings

curried cauliflower

Heat the oil in a large, heavy saucepan over medium-high heat. Add the onion and bay leaf and sauté for 7 minutes or until the onion becomes golden brown. Add the garlic, cardamom, and curry powder, stir well, and sauté for 2 minutes. Lower the heat and add the cauliflower, sautéeing gently for 4 to 5 minutes, until the

- 1 tablespoon vegetable oil
- 1 large yellow onion, diced
- 1 medium bay leaf
- 1 clove garlic, minced
- 2 cardamom seeds, hulled and crushed
- 1 tablespoon curry powder
- 1 head cauliflower, broken into 1-inch florets
- 1 large tomato, peeled, cored, seeded, and diced
- ½ cup Chicken Stock (see page 181)
- ¼ teaspoon freshly ground black pepper
- Salt to taste

stems of the cauliflower take on a glassy appearance. Add the tomato and sauté for 2 minutes. Add the chicken stock, pepper, and salt, and cook for an additional 5 minutes. Remove the pan from the heat, adjust seasoning, and serve with Red Rice with Diced Bananas and Mango Shake.

mango shake

I LIKE TO SERVE this refreshing shake with all kinds of curried foods. Papaya or cantaloupe may be substituted for the mango.

- 4 large, very ripe mangoes, peeled
- 2 cups skim milk
- 2 cups plain yogurt
- 4 sprigs fresh mint

Cut the mangoes into halves and remove the flesh from the large center seed. Discard the seed. Place the mango pulp in a blender with the milk and yogurt. Mix on high speed for 1 minute. Serve in 4 tall glasses over crushed ice. Garnish each glass with a sprig of mint.

Brown Rice with Peaches

IN LOUISIANA bay leaves are not removed from a dish before serving, and it is considered good luck to find one in your portion. In this recipe I extend the tradition to include cardamom pods in addition to bay leaf.

- 1 cup short-grain brown rice
- 1 tablespoon olive oil
- 1 medium-sized red Bermuda onion, peeled and finely diced
- 1 medium bay leaf
- 3 cardamom pods
- 2 cups Chicken Stock (see page 181)
- 3 large fresh peaches, seeds removed, flesh finely diced
- 12 fresh mint leaves, finely shredded
- Salt to taste
- Freshly ground black pepper to taste
- 4 whole-wheat pita breads

Place the rice in a colander and rinse under cold running water for 10 minutes. Drain.

Heat the oil over medium heat in a large, heavy saucepan. Add the onion and sauté for 3 minutes or until it is translucent. Add the bay leaf, cardamom, rinsed rice, and chicken stock, and bring to a boil. Reduce the heat and simmer, covered, for 30 to 45 minutes, until the liquid is absorbed.

Remove the pan from the heat and allow to sit, covered, for 10 minutes, until all of the stock is absorbed into the rice. Fold in the peaches and mint, season with salt and pepper, cover, and allow to stand for an additional 5 minutes.

Serve with warm pita bread.

4 main course or 6 side dish servings

Risotto with Sautéed Porcini Mushrooms

THE DELICATE FLAVOR of the porcini and the creaminess of the Arborio rice make this a wonderful main course or appetizer. Serve it with lots of crusty bread.

- ¾ cup Arborio rice (Italian short-grain rice sold at specialty food stores)
- 3 cups Chicken Stock (see page 181)
- 2 tablespoons extra-virgin olive oil
- ½ large yellow onion, peeled and finely chopped
- 1 large clove garlic, peeled
- 1 medium bay leaf
- 1 cup dry white wine or vermouth
- ¼ cup freshly grated Parmesan cheese, plus extra for serving, if desired
- 2 tablespoons freshly grated Romano cheese, plus extra for serving, if desired
- 1 tablespoon shredded fresh basil leaves
- Salt to taste
- Freshly ground black pepper to taste
- Sautéed Porcini Mushrooms (recipe follows)

Place the rice in a fine sieve and rinse under cold running water for 2 minutes. Drain.

Heat the chicken stock to a low simmer in a small saucepan and keep warm on the back of the stove.

Heat the oil in a large, heavy saucepan over moderately high heat. Add the onion, whole garlic clove, and bay leaf, and sauté until the onion is soft but not browned, about 2 minutes.

Add the rice to the pan and cook, stirring constantly, until the grains become translucent around the edges but are still white in the center, about 3 minutes. Immediately stir in the wine and reduce the heat to medium. Continue to stir until the wine is absorbed, then add 1 cup of the hot stock. Cook, stirring constantly, until the stock is absorbed. Continue stirring and adding stock in ½-cup portions, allowing each ½ cup to become fully absorbed before adding more, until the rice is tender yet retains its shape and is slightly al dente. This process will take approximately 15 minutes.

Remove the pan from the heat and discard the garlic clove and bay leaf. Fold in the Parmesan and Romano cheeses and basil. Season to taste with salt and pepper. Cover the pan and allow to sit for 2 minutes.

Spoon the risotto into individual serving bowls and top with the Sautéed Porcini Mushrooms. Serve immediately. Pass additional grated cheese at the table, if desired.

4 main course or 6 appetizer servings

sautéed porcini mushrooms

WHEN SHOPPING for porcini mushrooms, take a moment to make sure that their weight is fairly heavy relative to their size. Next check for worms by breaking open one of the caps. If worms are present they will be easy to spot.

If porcini are not available, substitute chanterelles.

Trim and discard the base of the porcini stems. Wash the mushrooms to remove any grit, then dry. Cut the caps into ⅛-inch-thick slices and cut the stems into ¼-inch slices.

- 1 pound fresh porcini mushrooms
- 1 tablespoon extra-virgin olive oil
- 2 shallots, peeled and finely chopped
- 2 tablespoons dry white wine or vermouth
- Salt to taste
- Freshly ground black pepper to taste
- 1 tablespoon finely chopped fresh flat-leaf parsley leaves, for garnish

Heat the oil in a heavy skillet over moderately high heat. Add the shallots and sauté, stirring constantly, until translucent, about 2 minutes. Add the mushrooms and cook for an additional 2 minutes until they begin to soften. Stir in the wine, season with salt and pepper, and cook for 1 minute.

Remove the mushrooms from the pan and divide among the portions of risotto. Garnish with chopped parsley and serve immediately.

Risotto with Saffron and Dried Cherries

IN THIS RECIPE I match the sweetness of saffron and cherries with Arborio rice. Any dried fruit, such as blueberries, cranberries, or red currants, can be substituted for the cherries.

- 6 to 8 cups Chicken Stock (see page 181)
- 4 tablespoons extra-virgin olive oil
- Pinch of saffron threads
- 1 large yellow onion, peeled and finely chopped
- 2 cups Arborio rice (Italian short-grain rice sold at specialty food stores)
- 1 cup dry white wine
- Salt to taste
- Freshly ground black pepper to taste
- 1 cup dried cherries

Place the chicken stock in a large saucepan and heat to a simmer. Keep warm on the back of the stove.

Heat the oil in a large, heavy saucepan over moderately high heat. Add the saffron, stir for 1 minute to release the flavor into the oil, then add the onion. Sauté until the onion is soft but not browned, about 2 minutes. Add the rice to the pan and cook, stirring constantly, until the grains become translucent around the edges but are still white in the center, about 3 minutes. Immediately stir in the wine and reduce the heat to medium. Continue to stir until the wine is absorbed, then add 1 cup of the hot stock. Cook, stirring constantly, until the stock is absorbed. Continue stirring and adding stock in ½-cup portions, allowing each ½ cup to become fully absorbed before adding more, until the rice is tender yet retains its shape and is slightly al dente. (This will take about 15 minutes.)

Remove the pan from the heat and season with salt and pepper. Cover the pan and allow to sit for 2 minutes, then fold in the cherries.

Spoon the risotto into bowls and serve immediately.

4 to 6 appetizer or dessert servings

Pumpkin Seed Parmesan Risotto

SPRINKLING THE Parmesan risotto with pumpkin seeds and passing it under the broiler before serving gives the top layer a wonderful smooth-crunchy texture.

Place the chicken stock in a large saucepan and heat to a simmer. Keep warm on the back of the stove.

Heat the oil in a large, heavy saucepan over moderately high heat. Add the onion and bay leaf and sauté until the onion is soft but not browned, about 2 minutes. Add the rice to the pan and cook, stirring constantly, until the grains become translucent around the edges but are still white in the center, about 3 minutes. Immediately stir in the wine and reduce the heat to medium. Continue to stir until the wine is absorbed, then add 1 cup of the hot stock. Cook, stirring constantly, until the stock is absorbed. Continue stirring and adding stock in ½-cup portions, allowing each cup to become fully absorbed before adding more, until the rice is tender yet retains its shape and is slightly al dente. (This will take about 15 minutes.)

Remove the pan from the heat and discard the bay leaf. Fold in ½ cup of the Parmesan and season with salt and pepper. Cover the pan and allow to sit for 2 minutes.

Spoon the risotto into individual heatproof serving bowls or one large heatproof bowl and top with the remaining Parmesan. Place the bowl(s) under a broiler for 30 seconds to melt the cheese. Remove from the oven. Top each serving with pumpkin seeds, place under the broiler, and allow to cook to a light golden brown, about 30 seconds. Serve immediately.

6 appetizer or 4 main course servings

- 6 to 8 cups Chicken Stock (see page 181)
- 4 tablespoons extra-virgin olive oil
- 1 large yellow onion, peeled and finely chopped
- 1 medium bay leaf
- 2 cups Arborio rice (Italian short-grain rice sold at specialty food stores)
- 1 cup dry white wine
- Salt to taste
- Freshly ground black pepper to taste
- 1 cup freshly grated Parmesan cheese
- 1 cup toasted pumpkin seeds (use the spicy variety if desired)

Sweet Risotto with Grilled Pineapple and Mango

For variation, add chopped nuts, dried fruit, or a dollop of Mascarpone cheese to the risotto before serving.

To slice the mangoes, hold one in your hand with the thick base of the fruit on a cutting board. With a sharp knife, slice vertically down both sides of the fruit and remove the 2 elliptical disks of fruit on either side of the large seed. Holding a disk of fruit flat on a cutting board, being careful not to cut all the way through the mango skin, make a series of criss-cross incisions into the meat so that a diamond pattern is cut into it. Repeat with each mango disk (4 in all) and set aside.

Place the rice in a fine sieve and rinse under cold running water for 2 minutes. Drain.

In a heavy saucepan, combine the milk, sugar, butter (if

- 2 mangoes
- ½ cup Arborio rice (Italian short-grain rice sold at specialty food stores)
- 2 cups whole milk
- ¼ cup sugar
- 2 tablespoons unsalted butter (optional)
- 1 vanilla bean, split lengthwise to expose seeds
- 1 egg yolk (optional)
- 1 pineapple, peeled, cored, and cut into ½-inch slices

using), and vanilla bean. Bring to a low boil and add the rice. Simmer gently, stirring continuously to keep the rice from sticking to the sides of the pan, until the rice is cooked through, about 15 minutes. Add the egg yolk, if desired, to give the risotto a thicker, creamier texture. Remove the pan from the heat, discard the vanilla bean, and cover to keep warm.

Preheat the grill until the coals are white-hot. Place the pineapple slices on the grill until seared with definite grill marks, about 3 to 5 minutes per side. Remove the slices and keep warm. Place the mango slices on the grill, flesh side down, and sear for no longer than 2 to 3 minutes.

Place the risotto in decorative serving bowls, arranging warm grilled fruit on plates around the bowls. Serve immediately.

4 to 6 appetizer or dessert servings

Hazelnut Rice Raviolis with Gorgonzola

THESE RAVIOLIS WILL turn out even better if the risotto is made a day in advance, as after a night in the refrigerator the risotto will be easier to form into the "cups" into which the cheese is placed.

- *2 cups Chicken Stock (see page 181)*
- *⅓ cup virgin olive oil*
- *½ large yellow onion, peeled and finely chopped*
- *1 medium bay leaf*
- *1 cup Arborio rice (Italian short-grain rice sold at specialty food stores)*
- *½ cup dry white wine*
- *Pinch of basil*
- *Pinch of thyme*
- *Pinch of nutmeg*
- *1 egg yolk*
- *½ cup heavy cream*
- *¼ cup freshly grated Parmesan cheese*
- *¼ cup Gorgonzola cheese*
- *1 whole egg*
- *2 cups whole milk*
- *1 cup ground hazelnuts*

Heat the chicken stock in a small saucepan over medium heat. Cover, remove from the heat, and keep warm.

Heat 1 tablespoon of the oil in a large, heavy saucepan over high heat. Add the onion and bay leaf and sauté until the onion is soft, about 3 minutes. Add the rice and sauté until it takes on a glassy appearance, about 2 minutes. Add the wine, basil, thyme, and nutmeg, and stir well. Slowly add 1 cup warm chicken stock, lower the heat to a simmer, and cook for 5 to 6 minutes, stirring constantly. Add the remaining stock and cook for 12 to 13 minutes, stirring constantly. Remove the pan from the heat and allow to cool slightly, uncovered, for 2 to 3 minutes.

Beat the egg yolk and cream together in a small bowl and add to the rice, mixing well. Add the Parmesan cheese. Pour the risotto onto a tray or baking sheet and set aside to cool completely.

When the risotto is cool, divide it into 12 equal parts and roll into balls. Moisten your hands with water and place 1 risotto ball into the center of 1 cupped hand, spreading the rice with your other hand to form a hollow cavity. (Keep your fingers moist so the rice will not stick to them.) Place 1 teaspoon Gorgonzola cheese into the hollowed cavity in the rice and enclose it completely by pinching the rice together. You now have a rice ball stuffed with Gorgonzola. To form the ravioli, gently press the ball into a disk shape between both hands, then set aside on the tray. Repeat with the remaining rice balls and cheese.

To make an egg wash, beat together the egg and milk in a small bowl. Place the hazelnuts on a flat tray or dish. Dip each rice ravioli into the egg wash, then into the ground hazelnuts, pressing gently to make sure the nuts stick. Set aside on a clean dish.

Preheat the oven to 375° F.

Heat the remaining oil in a large, heavy nonstick skillet over medium heat. Gently sauté the ravioli until golden brown, about 2 minutes per side. Transfer the cooked ravioli to a baking sheet and cook for an additional 5 minutes in the oven. Remove from the oven and drain on kitchen towels. Serve immediately.

6 appetizer or 4 main course servings

WILD RICE

Native to the northern United States and southern Canada, this aquatic grass seed (not a grain at all) is believed to have been part of the Native American diet up to ten thousand years ago. Nutty and rich in flavor and boasting a pleasant chewiness, wild rice is traditionally harvested by canoeing into wetlands, bending the grass (which can grow up to 8 feet tall) into the canoe, and then either knocking off the seeds with the canoe paddles or shaking them off by hand. Not surprisingly, many companies choose not to engage in this traditional method and have figured out ways to cultivate wild rice in a much less laborious manner: They grow the rice in commercial diked paddies using hybrid seeds, chemicals, and mechanized sowing and harvesting methods. If you are interested in trying truly wild rice, read the label carefully to find out how it was grown and harvested.

Though wild rice tends to be expensive, it can be stretched by combining it with brown rice or other less costly grains. It provides double the protein of true rice and higher levels of B vitamins. I like adding dried fruit, such as cherries or apricots, to wild rice 5 minutes before it is finished cooking.

Wild Rice with Blood Oranges and Leek Rondels

- 1 cup long-grain wild rice
- 2½ cups Chicken Stock (see page 181)
- 1 medium bay leaf
- 1 tablespoon orange zest
- 1 clove
- ¼ teaspoon salt
- ¼ teaspoon freshly ground black pepper
- 2 leeks, washed and trimmed
- 4 blood oranges, peeled
- 1 tablespoon canola oil
- 1 teaspoon sugar

Place the rice in a fine sieve and pick over to remove any foreign objects. Rinse well under cold running water. Drain.

Bring the stock to a boil in a large, heavy saucepan. Add the rice, bay leaf, orange zest, clove, salt, and pepper. Reduce to a simmer and cook, uncovered, for 45 minutes to 1 hour. (Be attentive to the rice during the last few minutes of cooking. Some of the grains will burst open, which does not indicate that they are overcooked. The rice should have a nutty bite to it when cooked.) Drain any extra cooking liquid. Cover and let stand for 10 minutes.

Cut the leeks into crosswise rounds, about 1/16 inch thick. Segment the oranges over a bowl, reserving any juice that may fall into the bowl.

Heat the oil in a large sauté pan over medium-high heat. Add the leeks and sauté for 2 minutes. Add the oranges and sauté for an additional 1 minute. Add any reserved orange juice and the sugar, stirring well. Allow the mixture to cool slightly, then fold into the wild rice and serve.

4 main course or 6 side dish servings

PASTA

Although the exact origin of pasta is unknown, it is likely that it evolved in many places at the same time. The Chinese probably ate noodles as long ago as 5000 B.C., and the Etruscans were enjoying pasta on land that is now Italy around 400 B.C. If the Venetian explorer Marco Polo actually did carry pasta to Italy from China in 1295, it was most likely to compare it to the pasta in his homeland, not to introduce it as a new dish. In the late 1700s Thomas Jefferson tasted pasta in Naples and brought the idea back to the United States, but it didn't really catch on until the nineteenth century when Italian immigrants arrived in America with the dried pastas that are so popular today.

There are countless ways to serve pasta, although the different shapes lend themselves to particular types of sauces and accompaniments. The thicker pastas are generally paired with heavier sauces. For instance, penne, ziti, rigatoni, and the ear-shaped orecchiette take well to chunky meat or pulpy vegetable sauces such as the tomato-based puttanesca. The thick noodles, such as fettuccine or pappardelle, go with rich meat or cream sauces. Wider noodles, such as lasagne, and heavier shapes also stand up well to baking in casseroles. Finer pasta (e.g., angel hair and vermicelli) are matched with lighter or thinner sauces to keep the strands separate and lightly coated. A good example is spaghetti simply tossed with garlic, olive oil, and parsley or chopped tomatoes and basil.

An additional category of pasta becoming increasingly popular in the United States is Asian noodles. This includes the Japanese soba (made with buckwheat and sometimes wheat flour) and udon (made with whole-wheat flour sometimes lightened with brown rice flour), noodles that are generally eaten in hot broth or served chilled with a dipping sauce. Chinese bean thread and rice noodles are also gaining favor. Bean thread noodles are often stir-fried or braised with other ingredients; fresh rice noodles are generally used to make dumplings, while dried rice noodles, which are very thin, are added to salads and soups.

Basic Pasta

FOR ADDED FLAVOR, add fresh herbs to this basic dough: Blanch the herbs in boiling water for a few seconds (to release the oils), then shock in ice water and drain before working into the dough.

Leftover pasta dough can be frozen, well-wrapped, for months. When ready to use, defrost and knead lightly before rolling.

- 1 pound semolina flour (see Note)
- 6 whole eggs
- 1 tablespoon extra-virgin olive oil
- Pinch of salt
- Pinch of freshly ground black pepper
- Approximately 6 tablespoons ice water

Sift the flour into a large bowl and make a well in the center. Place the eggs, oil, salt, and pepper in the well and, using a fork or your fingertips, lightly blend the ingredients until evenly moistened. Add the cold water as needed, a little at a time, to form a smooth dough. Turn the dough out onto a lightly floured surface. Gather into a ball and place in a clean bowl. Cover with a damp cloth and refrigerate for at least 30 minutes or until ready to use.

Using a pasta machine, roll and cut the dough into the desired shape, according to the manufacturer's instructions.

Note: For a nuttier flavor, use $\frac{1}{3}$ pound amaranth flour and $\frac{2}{3}$ pound semolina flour.

Makes 2 pounds of dough

Linguine with Caraway and Minted Pea Purée

I LIKE TO USE dried peas (as well as beans) to make flavorful sauces that are low in fat. For this recipe, I chose dried marrowfat peas, which are large and full of earthy flavor, but any dried pea can be substituted.

In a heavy saucepan, combine the peas, onion, and chicken stock, and bring to a boil over high heat. Reduce the heat to low and simmer, covered, for 30 minutes. Stir in the caraway seeds and continue to cook for an additional 30 minutes. Remove the pan from the heat.

Place the pea mixture in a blender or food processor. Add the mint and 1 tablespoon of the olive oil and purée on high speed for 1 minute. Adjust seasoning with salt and pepper, return the purée to the saucepan, and cover to keep warm.

Bring a large pot of water to a boil over high heat and add 1 teaspoon salt, the remaining tablespoon olive oil, and the linguine. Cook the linguine, stirring occasionally to separate the strands, until al dente, about 8 minutes. Drain the linguine, then toss with the minted pea purée. Serve immediately.

4 main course servings

- *1 cup dried marrowfat peas*
- *¼ small yellow onion, peeled and finely shredded*
- *2 cups Chicken Stock (see page 181)*
- *10 caraway seeds*
- *¼ cup shredded fresh mint leaves*
- *2 tablespoons extra-virgin olive oil*
- *Salt to taste*
- *Freshly ground black pepper to taste*
- *1 pound linguine*

Soba Noodles with Citrus and Smoked Shrimp

I FIND THAT soba noodles absorb the flavor of sauces, broths, and other seasonings much better than wheat- or rice-based noodles. Although any type of orange can be used in this recipe, blood oranges will make for the most attractive presentation.

Over a stainless steel mixing bowl, carefully segment the fruit, retaining any juice that may fall into the bowl with the segments.

Bring 2 quarts of salted water to a rolling boil in a large, heavy pot. Add the soba noodles, stirring occasionally to prevent sticking, and cook until tender, about 4 minutes. Drain the noodles into a colander, then refresh by immersing in a pot of ice water. Drain, then place in the bowl with the fruit segments and juice.

Heat the oil in a skillet over medium heat. Add the garlic and sauté for 2 minutes. Add the cilantro and tamari, stirring well. Remove from the heat and allow to cool. Combine the tamari mixture with the noodles and toss well to coat. Divide the noodles among 4 serving plates.

In a separate bowl, gently toss together the shrimp, scallions, and cucumber. Place on top of the noodle portions and serve immediately.

4 appetizer or 2 main course servings

- *2 oranges, peeled*
- *2 limes, peeled*
- *1 lemon, peeled*
- *1 7-ounce package soba (buckwheat) noodles*
- *1 tablespoon virgin olive oil*
- *1 large clove garlic, minced*
- *1 teaspoon chopped fresh cilantro leaves*
- *1 teaspoon tamari*
- *4 ounces smoked shrimp (smoked salmon may be substituted), chopped into ½-inch pieces*
- *4 scallions, whites and greens, thinly sliced on the diagonal*
- *½ cup seeded, shredded cucumber*

Soba Noodles with Shiitake Mushrooms and Scallions

THE BEST soba noodles are made with buckwheat flour only, rather than a combination of buckwheat and wheat flours. For variation in this recipe, fold shredded apples or peaches into the noodles before serving.

- 1 7-ounce package soba (buckwheat) noodles
- 4 tablespoons sesame oil
- 1 tablespoon tamari
- 10 shiitake mushrooms, stems discarded, finely sliced
- 3 large scallions, whites and greens, thinly sliced on the diagonal
- ½ pound fresh spinach leaves, washed, dried, and stems removed

Bring 3 quarts salted water to a rolling boil in a heavy pot. Add the noodles and 1 tablespoon of the sesame oil and cook for 3 to 4 minutes, stirring occasionally, until the noodles are al dente.

Drain the noodles into a colander, then refresh by immersing in a pot of ice water. Drain and toss in a large bowl with 1 tablespoon of the sesame oil and the tamari. Mix gently to avoid breaking the noodles. Set aside at room temperature.

In a small sauté pan, heat the remaining 2 tablespoons oil over medium-high heat. Add the mushrooms and sauté for 2 minutes. Remove from the heat and fold in the scallions. Toss with the soba noodles and serve over crisp spinach leaves.

4 appetizer or 2 main course servings

Nuts and Seeds

PEANUTS

The peanut is the high-protein seed of a small vine-type plant that sends its pods underground to ripen and mature. Though considered a nut, it is, rather, a legume belonging to the same family as the pea.

Many historians believe that peanuts originated in Peru and that the Portuguese slave traders carried peanuts from Brazil to Africa, planting them on the West African coast so that they would have an inexpensive way of feeding their African captives while they waited to board ships to the New World.

While in the United States peanuts are generally considered a snack food and are the key ingredient in peanut butter (created in 1890 by a St. Louis physician to treat invalids and elderly patients, today peanut butter accounts for nearly half the United States peanut harvest), in other parts of the world it is treated more as a vegetable. In Africa and Indonesia, peanuts are ground and used to enrich soups and sauces; in Indonesia and China they are used whole in savory dishes.

Three main types of peanuts are cultivated in the United States: Runners, which were introduced in the 1970s, are the newest type and are usually made into peanut butter; Virginia peanuts are commonly roasted in their shells; and Spanish peanuts, which are smaller and rounder than the other two types, are used in peanut butter and in candy and are also sold shelled and salted.

Peanuts are slightly higher in protein than other nuts and are a smidgen lower in fat (though they are still a high-fat food).

PAGE 150

Top, left to right:

walnuts, pine nuts

Middle: black sesame seeds,

almonds

Bottom: pistachios,

white sesame seeds

PAGE 151

Top, left to right:

hazelnuts, macadamia nuts

Bottom: peanuts, granola

Peanut Soup

Peanut Soup can be found throughout Asia and Africa. To vary this recipe, sprinkle the soup with ground coconut along with the cilantro. If desired, use the Cajun Peanut Butter from page 155 in this recipe.

Cut a 6-inch square of muslin and into it place all ingredients except the stock, peanut butter, rice, and cilantro. Gather up the sides of the muslin to form a purse and tie tightly with a piece of string.

Place the stock in a large, heavy pot and add the muslin bag. Bring to a boil over high heat, then reduce to a simmer and cook, covered, for 1 hour.

- *2 stalks lemon grass, crushed and folded or tied into a bow*
- *2 cloves garlic, peeled and crushed*
- *1 red chili pepper, seeds and stems removed, diced*
- *2 tablespoons shredded coconut*
- *Segments of 1 lemon, finely diced*
- *1 teaspoon peeled and chopped ginger*
- *10 coriander seeds*
- *4 pods cardamom, crushed*
- *2 quarts Chicken Stock (see page 181)*
- *2 cups unsalted crunchy or smooth peanut butter*
- *1 cup cooked rice of your choice*
- *2 tablespoons minced fresh cilantro*

4 to 6 appetizer servings

Remove the pot from the heat and discard the muslin bag.

Place the peanut butter in a large mixing bowl and drizzle in enough stock to form a loose paste, stirring constantly. (It should be the consistency of heavy cream.) Slowly add the peanut stock back into the remaining stock, stirring constantly to incorporate. Return the stock to a low heat and simmer to warm, stirring.

Ladle the soup into serving bowls and top each portion with rice and cilantro.

Cajun Peanuts

FOR VARIATION, substitute other types of nuts, such as
walnuts, hazelnuts, or pecans, for the peanuts.

- 1 pound shelled raw peanuts
- ¼ egg white
- 2 tablespoons brown sugar
- 1 teaspoon salt
- ½ teaspoon freshly ground black pepper
- ¼ teaspoon cayenne pepper
- ¼ teaspoon paprika

Preheat the oven to 375° F.

Combine the peanuts and egg white in a large bowl. Sprinkle the peanuts with the remaining ingredients, mixing well. Lay the seasoned peanuts in a single layer on a large baking sheet lined with parchment paper and cook in the preheated oven until the brown sugar on the peanuts forms little crystals, about 15 minutes, watching closely to make sure they don't burn. Remove the peanuts from the oven, separate, and cool. Store in an airtight container for up to 2 or 3 weeks.

Makes 1 pound

To make Cajun Peanut Butter: Omit the egg white and proceed with the recipe as directed. Purée the cooled peanuts to desired consistency in a food processor, approximately 1 minute for a smooth peanut butter, less time for chunky. Store in the refrigerator in an airtight container. Remember when making your own nut butters to prepare small amounts at a time, as unlike store-bought products, homemade butters contain no preservatives and have a short shelf life—about two weeks—even when refrigerated.

PISTACHIO NUTS

Pistachios grow on a deciduous evergreen tree, the nuts enclosed in their shells within wrinkled reddish fruits. One of the two nuts mentioned in the Old Testament (the other is the almond), pistachios were introduced in the United States in the 1880s. Interestingly, they didn't catch on until the 1930s, when importers started to dye them red (to attract attention as well as hide imperfections) and sell them from vending machines.

Pistachios split open as they ripen, making it easy to get to the tasty nut kernel. The most common ways to eat the nuts are directly from the shell (either in their natural state or roasted and salted) and in candies and desserts, such as Middle Eastern baklava (a honey-sweetened phyllo dough and nut pastry) and halvah (a confection made with sesame paste and honey). Pistachios are also used to thicken sauces as well as in pilafs, pâtés, and sausages, and can be made into a delicious nut butter.

One of my favorite pistachio recipes is pistachio milk: To make it, purée pistachios with skim mik, add cardamom and fresh mint or basil, and refrigerate for a few hours; strain the beverage before serving. In my experience the best pistachios come from Iran.

Pistachio Roasted Bananas with Clear Lime or Orange-Strawberry Sauce

THE COMBINATION of bananas, lime, and nuts gives this dish a Caribbean flavor. The nuts are soaked in milk prior to baking, which enhances their flavor and keeps them from drying out when heated in the oven.

At the beginning of the summer, when the strawberries at the market are at their peak of flavor, I replace the Clear Lime Sauce with Orange-Strawberry Sauce.

Preheat the oven to 350° F.

Soak the peeled nuts in the cold milk for 1 hour. Drain and

- 8 ounces shelled, unsalted natural (not red) pistachio nuts (walnuts or pecans may be substituted)
- 2 cups cold whole milk
- 6 whole bananas, just underripe
- Clear Lime Sauce or Orange-Strawberry Sauce (recipes follow)

dry on a clean towel. Chop the nuts roughly and place in a large shallow dish. Peel the bananas carefully to avoid breaking them. Gently press a peeled banana into the nuts, turning to coat completely. Place on an ungreased baking sheet. Repeat with the remaining bananas.

Bake the bananas for 10 to 12 minutes. Allow to cool, then carefully place on 6 individual serving plates, passing the Clear Lime Sauce or Orange-Strawberry Sauce on the side.

6 dessert servings

clear lime sauce

LEAVE THE VANILLA BEAN in the sauce until the sauce is completely finished. That way it will continue to impart its flavor for as long as possible.

Place all of the ingredients in a small saucepan and bring to

- ⅔ cup sugar
- 6 tablespoons water
- Grated zest and juice of 6 limes
- 1 vanilla bean, split lengthwise

a boil. Remove from the heat and allow to cool; the sauce will thicken as it cools. Stir and serve with Pistachio Roasted Bananas.

Makes ⅓ cup

orange-strawberry sauce

Place the strawberries in a mixing bowl and mash with a fork to a purée. Stir in the liqueur and mix well.

- 1 pint strawberries, washed, dried and diced
- ¼ cup Grand Marnier liqueur

Serve with Pistachio Roasted Bananas.

Makes 2½ cups

PINE NUTS

Pine nuts are the sweet and oily seeds of the cones of certain types of pine trees. To harvest the nuts, the pine cones are dried, which makes their scales spread apart, and the seeds, which can range from $\frac{1}{4}$ inch to 2 inches long depending on the type of tree they come from, are dislodged. The nutshells are then cracked to free the smooth, ivory-colored kernels inside. Because this process is labor-intensive, pine nuts tend to be expensive.

Pine nuts have been a staple in Mediterranean and South American cuisines as well as among Native Americans for centuries. They are also a standard ingredient in Korea, where they are added to such dishes as rice porridge, kim chee (spicy, pickled vegetables, often cabbage), candies, and glutinous rice desserts, and in China, where they may be incorporated into sweets or fried and used as a garnish. Pine nuts are a common ingredient in the Italian pesto sauce and, when toasted, make a satisfying addition to salads, couscous, and rice dishes.

Besides the culinary uses of this, unfortunately, high-fat nut, pine nuts have throughout history been endowed with curious magical powers: They were once believed to make the person who ate them bulletproof and have also been credited with the ability to cure gout, cataracts, and a number of cattle diseases.

Pine nuts are also known as pignoli, piñon nuts, Indian nuts, and stone nuts.

Pine Nut and Pistachio Relish

I ENJOY THE CRUNCHINESS of the pistachios combined with the smooth oiliness of the pine nuts in this variation of Mediterranean caponata. My favorite way to serve this relish is with a wedge of hard cheese, such as a Cheddar or

Cheshire, and crackers. It is also delicious served on top of rigatoni or as an accompaniment to grilled chicken.

Place the chopped eggplant in a colander and sprinkle with ¼ cup of the salt. Set aside and allow to "sweat" for 20 to 30 minutes.

Heat ½ cup of the olive oil in a large, heavy saucepan over medium-high heat. Add the onions and garlic and sauté until translucent. Add the tomatoes, basil, oregano, and thyme, and sauté for 5 to 8 minutes. Remove from the heat.

Bring 4 cups water to a boil in a small pot. Add the chopped celery and blanch for 1 minute. Remove the celery with a slotted spoon and add to the tomato mixture. Repeat the blanching process with the olives.

- 1 large eggplant, peeled and finely chopped
- ¼ cup plus ½ teaspoon salt
- 1 cup virgin olive oil
- 1 medium yellow onion, peeled and finely chopped
- 3 large cloves garlic, peeled and minced
- 8 large tomatoes, peeled, seeded, and diced
- 1 tablespoon minced fresh basil
- 1 tablespoon minced fresh oregano
- ½ teaspoon minced fresh thyme
- 6 stalks celery, trimmed and finely chopped
- 1 cup green olives, pits removed and flesh finely chopped
- 1 cup toasted pine nuts
- 1 cup shelled, unsalted natural (not red) pistachio nuts, outer skins removed
- ½ cup red wine vinegar
- ¾ cup sugar
- Freshly ground black pepper to taste

Thoroughly rinse the salt from the eggplant under cold running water and drain on paper towels.

Heat the remaining olive oil in a heavy saucepan over medium-high heat. Add the eggplant and sauté for 3 minutes, then fold in the pine nuts and pistachios. Remove the pan from the heat and allow to cool slightly. Combine the eggplant and tomato mixtures.

In a small saucepan, heat the vinegar and sugar over low heat, stirring to dissolve the sugar, about 4 minutes. Allow the mixture to cool, then add to the eggplant-tomato relish.

Adjust seasonings to taste.

Serve warm or at room temperature. Pine Nut and Pistachio Relish can be refrigerated for several days.

Makes 1 quart

Tahini Dip

SESAME SEEDS

Sesame seeds, the tiny, flat seeds of a tall tropical plant, are among the world's oldest seasonings. They are native to India and were carried to the United States by slaves from Africa, who called them benné seeds. Though they exist in shades of red, black, and brown, the easiest to come by are ivory-colored. Extremely high in calcium when unhulled (which means the bran has not been removed), they play a significant role in many cuisines, including those of Africa, India, Japan, China, Korea, and the Middle East. In Japan, China, and Korea the oil produced from sesame seeds is used for cooking and as a flavoring. In the Middle East sesame seeds are a common addition to breads, and tahini (sesame seed paste) is an integral ingredient in dips, such as hummus bi tahina *(tahini and chick-peas) and* baba ghanoush *(tahini and eggplant) as well as the classic sweet called* halvah *(ground sesame seeds combined with honey and sometimes dried fruit and nuts). A similar but drier paste made with toasted sesame seeds is used as a sauce for cold noodle and chicken dishes and in marinades in the Sichuan province of China.*

To bring out the flavor of sesame seeds, toast them briefly in a dry skillet before using in a recipe.

I LIKE TO SERVE this Middle Eastern specialty as a dip with fresh vegetable crudités or as a dressing on chilled pasta.

• *½ cup tahini (sesame seed paste)*	• *3 tablespoons chopped fresh cilantro leaves*
• *¼ cup dried roasted unsalted cashew nuts, very finely chopped*	• *2 tablespoons warm water*
• *1 tablespoon toasted sesame seeds*	• *1 tablespoon sesame oil*
• *2 tablespoons Roasted Garlic purée (see page 181)*	• *Dash of Worcestershire sauce*
	• *1 teaspoon crushed green peppercorns*
• *3 tablespoons fresh lemon juice*	• *Dash of Tabasco*
	• *Pinch of cumin*

Combine all of the ingredients in a bowl and mix well to incorporate. Chill and serve.

Makes 1½ cups

WALNUTS

For the ancient Romans the walnut was a symbol of the human brain and, based on the belief of that time that the shape of plants and their parts indicated how they could be used, they were also considered a cure for headaches. (Based on the same theory but in a reversal of interpretation, in the Middle Ages, walnuts were believed to induce headaches.) Because these nuts came to them via Persia, the ancient Romans called their walnuts Persian nuts; similarly, when this same species of nut reached America, by way of Britain, they were dubbed English walnuts.

English (Persian) walnuts are by far the most prevalent type of walnut in American markets; today, California is the world's leading producer. Also available but in limited quantities are black walnuts, which grow on a native North American tree. Black walnuts have such hard outer shells and hulls that crushing them requires mammoth pressure (some people run over them with their car tires in order to crack them). In the process, the nut meats are crushed to the point where they are mixed into the broken pieces of hull and shell and then must be picked out. Black-walnut devotees believe the extra effort pays off in superior flavor.

A delicious but expensive product of walnuts is walnut oil, the best of which is made in France. The oil is wonderful in salad dressings, either on its own or with a high-quality cider, white wine, or malt vinegar.

Before cooking or eating shelled walnuts, soak them in cold milk for about 20 minutes, then rinse them off with water and dry them. This process rehydrates the nuts and enhances their flavor.

Pickled Walnuts

THE TECHNIQUE FOR MAKING this very English treat goes back to medieval times when pickling was a common way of storing foods for the winter. Soft and chewy yet crisp, pickled walnuts have a unique flavor that is very hard to describe. I particularly enjoy these nuts as an afternoon snack with cheese from my native Cheshire.

To make this recipe you must have walnut trees of your own or a source for picking, as unripe walnuts are not available in stores. Always wear gloves when working with green walnuts because their juice stains the skin.

- *Green unhardened walnuts (see Note)*
- *½ cup salt for each quart of water needed to cover the walnuts*
- *White vinegar to cover the walnuts*

To each quart of vinegar, allow:
- *2 tablespoons black peppercorns*
- *2 tablespoons allspice*
- *1 teaspoon salt*
- *1 teaspoon sugar*

Make a strong brine by combining the necessary amount of warm water to cover the walnuts with ½ cup salt for each quart of water used. Allow the brine to cool.

Prick the walnuts well with a steel fork or large darning needle. Put them into a large earthenware bowl or pan and cover with the cool brine. Stir the walnuts 2 or 3 times daily for 6 days, then drain and cover with fresh brine. Let them sit for another 3 days, stirring 2 or 3 times daily, then drain. Spread the walnuts on large dishes or baking sheets and place in the sun until quite black, 2 to 3 days.

Sterilize enough jars to hold the walnuts, and fill each three fourths of the way to the top with walnuts.

Into a large heavy pot, place a sufficient amount of white vinegar to cover the walnuts along with the peppercorns, allspice, salt, and sugar, and boil over high heat for 15 minutes. Remove from the heat and allow to cool. When the vinegar mixture is quite cold, pour over the walnuts in their jars.

Secure the lids of the jars and store in a cool, dry place for up to several months.

Note: You must pick the berries before the wood of the walnuts begins to form (usually in the late summer). No amount of pickling after the wood has formed will soften the hard outer shells.

Walnut Scones

NUTS AND SEEDS

THIS IS A SIMPLE adaptation of the afternoon tea scone. If you want to expand the flavor a bit, add 1 ounce chopped candied ginger to the dough along with the walnuts.

Place the butter, 2 tablespoons of the sugar, the maple syrup, and salt in the bowl of a mixer fitted with a dough hook or paddle and cream on medium speed for 4 to 5 minutes. Alternatively, cream these ingredients with a hand-held electric mixer.

Sift together the flour and baking powder. Slowly add 1 cup of the flour to the creamed butter on low speed. Turn off the machine and scrape down the side of the bowl. On low speed, add the buttermilk, 3 eggs, one at a time, and the vanilla. Before the milk and eggs are completely incorporated, add the remaining flour and the walnuts, being very careful not to overmix. As soon as the flour and nuts have been mixed in and there is no "loose" flour, remove the batter from the bowl and chill in the refrigerator for 2 hours.

Grease two large baking sheets and set aside.

Place the batter on a lightly floured surface and roll into a rectangle between ½ inch and ¾ inch thick. Cut into scones with a 3-inch round cookie cutter and place on the greased baking sheets. Push the leftover scraps of dough together, roll out, and cut into scones with the cutter. Place the scones on the baking sheet in the refrigerator to chill for 45 minutes.

Preheat the oven to 375° F.

Make an egg wash with the remaining egg and 1 tablespoon water. Brush the tops of the scones with the egg wash and sprinkle lightly with the remaining 2 tablespoons sugar.

Bake the scones for 20 to 25 minutes or until golden brown. Cool on a wire rack and serve either hot or at room temperature with the unsalted butter, jams, and/or whipped cream. Store at room temperature for up to 2 days or freeze in airtight containers.

Makes 2 dozen scones

- *1 stick (4 ounces) unsalted butter*
- *4 tablespoons sugar*
- *3 tablespoons maple syrup*
- *1 teaspoon salt*
- *2⅔ cups all-purpose flour*
- *1 tablespoon baking powder*
- *1 cup lowfat buttermilk*
- *4 whole eggs*
- *½ teaspoon vanilla*
- *⅔ cup chopped walnuts*
- *Unsalted butter, jams, and/or whipped cream, for serving*

OPPOSITE *Walnut Scones (left) and Hazelnut and Carrot Muffins*

Walnut Oatmeal Cookies

- ¾ cup canola oil
- ⅔ cup light brown sugar
- ⅓ cup granulated sugar
- 1 whole egg
- 1 cup all-purpose flour
- ⅛ teaspoon baking soda
- ½ teaspoon cinnamon
- ⅛ teaspoon salt
- Pinch of ground cloves
- Pinch of nutmeg
- ⅔ cup rolled oats
- ¾ cup shelled, chopped walnuts
- ¼ cup honey
- 1 teaspoon pure vanilla extract

Preheat the oven to 375° F.

In a large mixing bowl, cream the oil, light brown and granulated sugars, and egg. Into a separate bowl, sift together the flour, baking soda, cinnamon, salt, cloves, and nutmeg, then add to the sugar mixture.

Fold in the oats and chopped walnuts, then add the honey and vanilla and mix for 2 minutes with your hands or a spoon, making sure the ingredients are well incorporated.

Line a baking sheet with parchment paper that has been lightly greased. Using a tablespoon, drop rounds of batter onto the sheet, leaving 1 inch between each spoonful. Bake the cookies for 15 to 20 minutes or until golden brown around the edges and evenly colored toward the center, then remove to a wire rack to cool. Serve warm.

Makes 24 to 30 cookies

OPPOSITE *Almond and Lemon Wafers (top) and Walnut Oatmeal Cookies*

HAZELNUTS AND FILBERTS

Hazelnuts (corylus avellana) are the fruit of a wild shrub. Filberts (corylus maxima), which grow on a small, related European tree, are larger and more robust and have a fringed husk. The distinction between hazelnuts and filberts is almost completely lost in the United States, where these two types of nuts are used interchangeably. Filberts, which were the second most widely consumed nuts during the Stone Age (beaten out by acorns for this honor), are named after a French abbot named St. Philbert, whose August feast day occurs at the same time that filberts ripen.

Toasting hazelnuts and filberts brings out their rich, sweet flavor and also makes it easier to remove their bitter, papery, brown skin. To remove the skin, rub the warm, toasted nuts in a dish towel. Hazelnuts and filberts can be used whole, chopped, or ground in desserts (they have a special affinity with chocolate) as well as in salads and savory dishes.

Hazelnut and Carrot Muffins

THESE MUFFINS have tremendous flavor and need not be reserved for breakfast—they make a great addition to dinner menus in place of bread.

• 1 cup plus 1 tablespoon vegetable oil	• ¼ cup Steen's syrup (a thick cane syrup available at grocery or specialty food stores) or blackstrap molasses
• 1½ cups cake flour	
• 1 teaspoon baking soda	
• ½ teaspoon baking powder	
• 1½ cups sugar	• ½ teaspoon pure vanilla extract
• ½ cup ground hazelnuts	• 2⅓ cups trimmed, peeled, and grated carrots
• ½ teaspoon cinnamon	
• 4 whole eggs	• 1 cup chopped skinned hazelnuts

Grease 12 4-ounce muffin cups with 1 tablespoon of the vegetable oil and preheat the oven to 350° F.

Sift the flour, baking soda, and baking powder into a bowl.

In a large bowl, using a tabletop mixer, combine the sugar and the remaining 1 cup vegetable oil. Add the ground hazelnuts, cinnamon, and flour mixture, and mix well. One at a time, add the eggs to the bowl, beating after each addition. Mix in the syrup and vanilla, then the carrots and chopped nuts. Mix on high speed for 1 minute or until all of the ingredients are well incorporated.

Divide the batter among the greased muffin cups and bake for 25 to 30 minutes or until golden brown and springy to the touch.

Remove the muffins from the pan and cool on a wire rack. Serve hot or store in airtight containers.

Makes 12 large muffins

Honey and Hazelnut Cakes with Minted Apricots

HERE I'VE CHOSEN rye flour rather than all-purpose flour as it gives the cakes a desirable grainy texture and a more interesting flavor. The apricots with which these cakes are served are a sort of old-fashioned compote. For variation, substitute 20 shredded organic rose petals for the mint.

- 12 dried apricots, seeded and finely chopped
- 20 fresh mint leaves, minced
- 1 cup honey
- ½ cup sugar
- ¼ teaspoon salt
- ¼ teaspoon baking soda
- 2 cups rye flour
- ¾ cup chopped unskinned hazelnuts
- ¼ cup dark rum
- 2 teaspoons anise powder
- ½ teaspoon cinnamon
- ¼ teaspoon powdered cloves
- ½ cup raisins

Mix together the apricots and mint in a small bowl and set aside.

Preheat the oven to 325° F. Line 12 muffin cups with paper baking liners and set aside.

Combine the honey and sugar in the top of a double boiler set over low heat. Cook, stirring constantly, until the sugar dissolves. Remove from the heat and pour the mixture into a large mixing bowl. Add the salt and baking soda, then slowly add the rye flour, stirring constantly. Add the hazelnuts, rum, anise, cinnamon, cloves, and raisins, stirring well.

Pour the batter into the muffin cups, filling them two thirds of the way to the top. Bake for 25 to 30 minutes in the preheated oven. Remove from the oven and allow to cool slightly before peeling off the paper liners. Serve the cakes warm with the minted apricots.

Makes 12 cakes

Plain Granola

FOR VARIATION, make your own no-bake cookies with this granola. To 1 pound of granola, add 2 ounces melted chocolate. Spoon out onto an ungreased baking sheet to form cookies. Make sure the granola and chocolate are the same temperature when you combine them, otherwise you'll end up with a large, lumpy mess.

- 1 pound rolled oats
- 1½ cups shelled, unsalted sunflower seeds
- 1½ cups slivered almonds
- 1 cup shredded coconut
- ¾ cup shelled, unsalted pumpkin seeds
- ½ cup pine nuts
- ½ cup shelled, unsalted pistachio nuts
- ½ cup shelled pecans, roughly chopped
- ¾ cup honey
- 1½ teaspoons pure vanilla extract

Preheat the oven to 325° F.

Place the dry ingredients in a large mixing bowl and combine well. Slowly stir in the honey and vanilla, making sure that each grain is evenly coated. Spread the granola mixture onto an ungreased baking sheet and bake for 20 minutes, or until the grains become crisp and very lightly browned, stirring every 5 minutes to prevent the granola from sticking to the pan and burning.

Remove the granola from the oven and allow to cool (it will get crunchier as it cools). Granola can be stored at room temperature in airtight containers or in the freezer in plastic bags.

Makes 4 pounds

Sweet Granola

WHEN COMBINED with raisins and other dried fruit, this granola makes a great energy-boosting snack.

- *1 stick (4 ounces) unsalted butter*
- *¾ cup honey*
- *½ cup brown sugar*
- *1½ teaspoons pure vanilla extract*
- *1 pound rolled oats*
- *1½ cups shelled, unsalted sunflower seeds*
- *1½ cups slivered almonds*
- *1 cup shredded coconut*
- *¾ cup shelled, unsalted pumpkin seeds*
- *½ cup pine nuts*
- *½ cup shelled, unsalted pistachio nuts*
- *½ cup shelled pecans, roughly chopped*

Preheat the oven to 325° F.

Place the butter, honey, sugar, and vanilla in a heavy, medium saucepan and melt over low heat until smooth.

Place the remaining ingredients in a large mixing bowl and combine well. Slowly stir in the butter mixture, making sure that each grain is evenly coated. Spread the granola mixture onto an ungreased baking sheet and bake for 25 minutes or until the grains are crisp and very lightly browned, stirring occasionally to prevent the mixture from sticking to the pan.

Remove the granola from the oven and allow to cool (it will get crunchier as it cools). Granola can be stored at room temperature in airtight containers or in the freezer in plastic bags.

Makes 4 pounds

MACADAMIA NUTS

Macadamia nuts are known today as a Hawaiian specialty, but they actually didn't arrive on the islands until the late nineteenth century and weren't cultivated there on a commercial level until 1949. For their earlier history, it is necessary to go to Australia, where a Dr. John Macadam is credited with discovering that the pale, round nuts we know today as macadamias were not only edible but singularly delicious: sweet, creamy, and rich. That good taste does, however, come at a price, as macadamias are higher in fat and calories than any other nut (on the positive side, they are also a good source of iron, magnesium, and thiamin).

Because macadamia nut shells are very hard and thick—it can take up to 300 pounds of pressure to crack them—they are usually sold preshelled. For this reason and because demand for these nuts exceeds supply, macadamias are fairly expensive.

Macadamia nuts are also known as Queensland nuts.

Macadamia Nut and Candied Orange Peel Florentine

IF YOU WANT to make this candy even more lavish, after cooling, paint the backs with melted chocolate, then store in a sealed container in the refrigerator until ready to serve.

Preheat the oven to 375° F.

Combine the cream, ⅓ cup of the butter, the sugar, corn syrup, and honey in a large, heavy saucepan and bring to a boil over high heat. Reduce the heat to a simmer and cook until it reaches 220° F on a candy thermometer (the edges of the batter will turn dark brown). To avoid crystallization while cooking, occasionally wash the sides of the pan with a pastry brush dampened with water. Remove the batter from the heat and allow to cool.

- ½ cup heavy cream
- ⅓ cup plus 1 tablespoon unsalted butter
- ½ cup sugar
- 2 tablespoons corn syrup
- 2 tablespoons honey
- ½ cup chopped macadamia nuts
- ¼ cup candied orange peel
- 1 tablespoon flour

In a small bowl, toss the nuts and orange peel in the flour and coat evenly. Gently mix the nuts and orange peel into the cooled batter.

Grease a large baking sheet with the remaining 1 tablespoon butter. Using a teaspoon, drop the batter onto the baking sheet, leaving 3 inches between each spoonful. Bake for 10 to 12 minutes, or until golden brown.

Remove the baking sheet from the oven and allow the candies to cool, then gently lift from the baking sheet.

Store in an airtight container until ready to serve.

Makes 2 dozen florentines

ALMONDS

Almonds are actually the seeds of a tree in the peach family. To see the family resemblance, crack open a peach pit and look at the kernel inside or, better yet, take a look at the fruit coating the almond on the tree— it is thin, green, and covered with a peachlike fuzzy down. Almonds are believed to have originated ages ago—almond remnants were identified at the Neolithic level beneath the palace of Knossos on the Greek island of Crete—and have over the years racked up an impressive list of interesting and entertaining uses and anecdotes. For example, the almond is one of two nuts mentioned in the Old Testament (the other is the pistachio); in the second century B.C., sugared almonds were distributed at joyous occasions, such as births and marriages; in the seventeenth century, the city of Nancy in northeastern France became famous for its almond macaroons, many of which were made by an order of nuns that came to be known as the Macaroon Sisters; and, to this day, in Sweden, the person who finds the almond hidden in the Christmas Eve rice pudding is supposedly destined to be the next at the table to be married.

Although there are two types of almonds—bitter and sweet—sale of the bitter ones, which have a stronger flavor, is illegal in the United States. This is because in their raw state bitter almonds contain a small amount of prussic acid, which is lethal in large doses. However, almond extracts and liqueurs made with bitter almonds can be sold in this country because the toxicity of their prussic acid is destroyed by the heat used in processing.

Almonds provide more calcium than any other nut and more dietary fiber than any other nut or seed. They are also good sources of iron, riboflavin, and vitamin E.

Almond and Lemon Wafers

I LIKE TO SERVE these wafers with vanilla ice cream, lemon sorbet, or fresh sliced fruit.

> • 2½ cups sugar
> • 2 cups ground almonds
> • 1 tablespoon all-purpose flour
> • 4 egg whites
> • Zest from 2 lemons
> • 1 tablespoon butter

Preheat the oven to 350° F.

In a large mixing bowl, combine the sugar, almonds, and flour. In a separate bowl and with a mixer on high speed, beat the egg whites until they form soft peaks. Carefully fold the egg whites into the sugar mixture, stirring only enough to blend, then add the lemon zest.

Lightly grease 2 baking sheets with the butter. Drop heaping teaspoons of batter onto the prepared baking sheets, leaving 3 inches between each one. With the back of a spoon, press each out into a thin disk, about 2 inches in diameter. Repeat until all of the batter is used. Place the filled baking sheets in the preheated oven and bake for about 10 minutes, or until light golden brown.

Remove the baking sheets from the oven and allow the wafers to cool before removing them from the sheet. Serve Almond and Lemon Wafers warm or store in an airtight container.

Makes 3 dozen wafers

Almond-Hazelnut Praline Paste

THIS PASTE can be used as a flavoring in many dishes: Stir it into slightly softened ice cream; place a teaspoon in the dripper of your coffee maker; or try an almond-hazelnut praline paste and jelly sandwich. For convenience, buy preshelled and peeled hazelnuts and almonds.

> • 2 pounds sugar
> • 2 cups water
> • 1½ pounds shelled and peeled hazelnuts
> • ½ pound shelled and peeled almonds
> • 1 tablespoon butter

Preheat the oven to 375° F.

In a large, heavy saucepan, combine the sugar and water and cook over medium heat until it becomes an amber-colored caramel. Remove from the heat.

Spread the nuts on an ungreased baking sheet and cook for 3 minutes in the preheated oven, then add to the caramel. Grease the baking sheet and a rolling pin with the butter. Pour the nut mixture out onto the greased baking sheet, then roll with the rolling pin to ensure an even thickness. Allow to cool.

When cool, break the praline into pieces and grind as finely as possible in a food processor set on high. (The finer you grind, the more oils released, making a better paste.)

Store the Almond-Hazelnut Praline Paste indefinitely in an airtight container in the refrigerator.

Makes 1 pound

Sprouting Your Own Seeds

THE TASTE OF SPROUTS varies depending upon the type of seed used. Try mung beans, mustard seeds, or alfalfa seeds and add them to salads, soups, sandwiches, and sautéed fish dishes.

Place ½ cup seeds in a colander or sieve and rinse well under running water, then drain. Soak a clean kitchen towel with water and place it on a shallow tray or baking dish. Sprinkle the seeds evenly over the wet cloth and place the tray in a dark place, such as in a closet or at the back of a kitchen cabinet. To keep bugs away, cover the sprouts with an inverted colander or a fine-meshed sieve. Make sure that during the entire sprouting process the cloth remains damp, rewetting it as necessary with fresh water.

Over the next few days, check the seeds to see if they have begun to sprout. The sprouts are usually ready to harvest after 3 days. To harvest, simply snip the sprouts with scissors along the stems as you would trim hair. (To increase the flavor of the harvested sprouts via photosynthesis, place them in direct sunlight 1 day prior to eating.)

Makes 2 cups

Vegetable Stock

USE THIS RECIPE as a loose guide for making vegetable stock. Depending on the flavor base you wish for your finished dish, choose other vegetables, such as turnips or bell peppers, in addition to or to the exclusion of the vegetables called for here. Or, for an even quicker stock base, retain the water used when boiling vegetables (such as potatoes or cabbage), then infuse it with whatever additional vegetables or herbs you wish. The wine can either be omitted using this technique, or it can be added at the last minute (after the vegetables are removed).

- ¼ cup olive oil
- 2 large yellow onions, peeled and roughly chopped
- 1 large carrot, washed and roughly chopped
- 1 large leek, washed and roughly chopped
- ½ head white cabbage, washed and roughly chopped
- 6 stalks celery, washed and roughly chopped
- 8 cloves garlic, peeled and roughly chopped
- 2 medium bay leaves
- 1 sprig fresh thyme
- 1 teaspoon white peppercorns
- 1 cup dry white wine (optional)

Heat the oil in a large, heavy stockpot over medium-high heat. Add all of the ingredients, stirring to mix well. Lower the heat, cover the pot, and cook very slowly until all of the vegetables are soft and without color, about 45 minutes, stirring occasionally.

Add 1 gallon water to the pot and bring to a boil. Reduce the heat and simmer for 15 minutes. Remove the pot from the heat and strain the stock into a clean container. Use right away or cool completely and freeze in 8-ounce portions for up to 3 months.

Makes 1 gallon

Chicken Stock

THIS STOCK may be covered and stored in the refrigerator for 1 week or frozen in small portions for up to 3 months.

- 4 pounds chicken bones
- 2 white onions, peeled and roughly chopped
- 2 medium bay leaves
- 1/2 head celery, trimmed and roughly chopped
- 2 leeks, white part only, thoroughly rinsed and roughly chopped
- 10 to 12 white peppercorns

Combine all of the ingredients in a large, heavy stockpot. Add 1 gallon water. Bring the mixture to a boil over high heat, skimming any scum that forms on the surface. Lower the heat and simmer, uncovered, for 1 hour, skimming any additional scum that forms on the surface.

Strain and cool.

Makes 3 quarts

Roasted Garlic

TO MAKE a great, simple dip, mash the garlic pulp, then add 1/2 tablespoon oil and 1/8 teaspoon each salt and pepper. Serve with toasted pita, sliced French bread, or crackers. To make a roasted Garlic Purée for use as a flavoring in other recipes, squeeze the garlic pulp into a blender, drizzle in a bit of olive oil, and blend until smooth.

- 2 whole heads garlic
- 1 tablespoon olive oil

Preheat the oven to 375° F.

Rub each head of garlic with olive oil and wrap tightly in aluminum foil. Bake in the oven until the garlic is soft to the touch, about 30 minutes.

Remove the foil packages from the oven and allow to sit until cool enough to handle. Unwrap the garlic. With a sharp knife, cut across the diameter of each garlic head and squeeze out the pulp into a small bowl. Use immediately or cover and store in the refrigerator for up to 2 days.

Makes approximately 1/4 cup

Mail-Order Sources

Many of the beans, grains, nuts, and seeds highlighted in this book are available at well-stocked grocery stores. Additional sources include health food, ethnic, and specialty food stores as well as the companies listed below.

Balducci's
424 Avenue of the Americas
New York, NY 10011
212-673-2600

Dean & Deluca
560 Broadway
New York, NY 10012
800-221-7714
212-431-1691

Deer Valley Farm
RD #1
Guilford, NY 13780
607-764-8556

Garden Spot Distributors
438 White Oak Road
New Holland, PA 17557
800-829-5100

Shiloh Farms
P. O. Box 97
Sulphur Springs, AR 72768-0097
501-298-3359

Walnut Acres
Penns Creek, PA 17862
800-433-3998

Whole Food Company
1705 Capital of Texas Highway South
Suite 400
Austin, TX 78746
512-328-7541
Whole Food Company maintains stores throughout the country. Call for a location near you.

Acknowledgments

I would like to thank the following people who have helped make this book possible:

Leslie Stoker, my publisher, for her constant encouragement and guidance

Melanie Falick, for her skillful editing and commitment to excellence

Trevor Wisdom Lawrence, for her help with recipe testing and writing

George Engel, Shane Gorringe, and Michael Felsenstein, for their assistance in the kitchen

Kathy Nada, for her patient administrative assistance

Ellen Silverman, for her stunning photography

Conversion Chart

BUTTER

Some confusion may arise over the measuring of butter and other hard fats. In the United States butter is generally sold in one-pound packages that contain four equal "sticks." The wrapper on each stick is marked to show tablespoons, so the cook can cut the stick according to the quantity required. The equivalent weights are:

1 stick = 115 g / 4 oz

1 tablespoon = 15 g / ½ oz

FLOUR

American all-purpose flour is milled from a mixture of hard and soft wheats, whereas British plain flour is made mainly from soft wheat. To achieve a near equivalent to American all-purpose flour, use half British plain flour and half strong bread flour.

SUGAR

In the recipes in this book, if sugar is called for it is assumed to be granulated, unless otherwise specified. American granulated sugar is finer than British granulated, closer to caster sugar, so British cooks should use caster sugar throughout.

INGREDIENTS AND EQUIPMENT GLOSSARY

The following ingredients and equipment are basically the same on both sides of the Atlantic, but have different names.

AMERICAN	BRITISH
arugula	rocket
baking soda	bicarbonate of soda
Belgian endive	chicory
bell pepper	sweet pepper (capsicum)
Bibb and Boston lettuce	soft-leaved, round lettuce
broiler/to broil	grill/to grill
cheesecloth	muslin
chile	chilli
cornstarch	cornflour
crushed hot red pepper	dried crushed red chilli
eggplant	aubergine
fava beans	broadbeans
heavy cream (37.6% fat)	whipping cream (35–40% fat)
hot pepper sauce	Tabasco sauce
kidney beans	red kidney beans
kitchen towel	tea towel
lima beans	butter beans
lowfat milk	semi-skimmed milk
parchment paper	nonstick baking paper
peanut oil	groundnut oil
pearl onion	button or baby onion
romaine lettuce	cos lettuce
Romano cheese	pecorino cheese
scallion	spring onion
shrimp	prawn (varying in size)
skillet	frying pan
tomato purée	sieved tomatoes or pasatta
whole milk	homogenized milk
zucchini	courgette

VOLUME EQUIVALENTS

These are not exact equivalents for the American cups and spoons, but have been rounded up or down slightly to make measuring easier.

AMERICAN MEASURES	METRIC	IMPERIAL
¼ t	1.25 ml	
½ t	2.5 ml	
1 t	5 ml	
½ T (1½ t)	7.5 ml	
1 T (3 t)	15 ml	
¼ cup (4 T)	60 ml	2 fl oz
⅓ cup (5 T)	75 ml	2½ fl oz
½ cup (8 T)	125 ml	4 fl oz
⅔ cup (10 T)	150 ml	5 fl oz (¼ pint)
¾ cup (12 T)	175 ml	6 fl oz
1 cup (16 T)	250 ml	8 fl oz
1¼ cups	300 ml	10 fl oz (½ pint)
1½ cups	350 ml	12 fl oz
1 pint (2 cups)	500 ml	16 fl oz
1 quart (4 cups)	1 litre	1¾ pints

OVEN TEMPERATURES

In the recipes in this book, only Fahrenheit temperatures have been given. Consult this chart for the Centigrade and gas mark equivalents.

OVEN	°F	°C	GAS MARK
very cool	250–275	130–140	½–1
cool	300	150	2
warm	325	170	3
moderate	350	180	4
moderately hot	375	190	5
	400	200	6
hot	425	220	7
very hot	450	230	8
	475	250	9

WEIGHT EQUIVALENTS

The metric weights given in this chart are not exact equivalents, but have been rounded up or down slightly to make measuring easier.

AVOIRDUPOIS	METRIC
¼ oz	7 g
½ oz	15 g
1 oz	30 g
2 oz	60 g
3 oz	90 g
4 oz	115 g
5 oz	150 g
6 oz	175 g
7 oz	200 g
8 oz (½ lb)	225 g
9 oz	250 g
10 oz	300 g
11 oz	325 g
12 oz	350 g
13 oz	375 g
14 oz	400 g
15 oz	425 g
1 lb	450 g
1 lb 2 oz	500 g
1½ lb	750 g
2 lb	900 g
2¼ lb	1 kg
3 lb	1.4 kg
4 lb	1.8 kg
4½ lb	2 kg

INDEX

Designed by Jim Wageman

Typefaces in this book are Erazure, designed by Jane Wyatt,
Dante, designed by Giovanni Mardersteig,
and Trajan, designed by Carol Twombley

The type was set by Laura Lindgren, New York City

Printed and bound by
Toppan Printing Company, Ltd.
Tokyo, Japan